CW01249999

Concept of Suffering in Buddhism

Indo-Tibetan Studies Series

Editor of the Series
Narendra Kumar Dash

Volume I : edited by Dr. N.K. Dash
Tibetan Studies : Past and Present

Volume II : edited by Prof. Pranabananda Jash
Perspective of Buddhist Studies
(Giuseppe Tucci Birth Centenary Volume)

Volume III : by Projit Kumar Palit
History of Religion in Tripura

Volume IV: edited by Narendra Kumar Dash
Concept of Suffering in Buddhism

Indo-Tibetan Studies Series-IV

Concept of Suffering in Buddhism

Edited by

Narendra Kumar Dash

2005

Kaveri Books

New Delhi - 110 002

© Editor

First Published in 2005
ISBN 81-7479-071-3

All rights reserved including the right to translate or to reproduce this book or parts thereof except brief passages for quotations in articles or critical reviews.

Published by : **Rakesh Goel**
Kaveri Books
4697/5-21A, Ansari Road,
New Delhi - 110 002 (India).
Tel.: 011 2328 8140, 2324 5799
e-mail: kaveribooks@vsnl.com

Laser Typesetting by : Aarati Computers, Delhi - 110 009.
Printed at : Chawla Offset Printers, Delhi - 110 052.

PRINTED IN INDIA

Preface

It is with greatpleasure that I introduce this book *Concept of Suffering in Buddhism*, the fourth volume in the Indo-Tibetan Studies Series. Indo-Tibetan Studies have long been common feature of Buddhist Studies at Vishva-Bharati, Santiniketan, founded by Rabindranath Tagore. The first Visiting Professor of this University, Professor Sylvan Levis took great personal interest in the growth and promotion of research work in Buddhism especially on comparative aspects. Aspiring young scholars were strongly encouraged to acquaint themselves with the Sanskrit and Pali originals of Buddhist literature as well as to read Tibetan and Chenise translations. Even since prof. Levi, a number of noted, eminent scholars, both Indian and foreign, contributed considerably to the steady growth of Indo-Tibetan/ Buddhist studies.

In the fast developing, economically and technically progressing and progressive world of ours the concept of suffering seems to be out of place. More does not want to think of soxnow and suffering, let alone under go them! Man always longs for peace and happiness. However, a close look at modern man's insecure and ense, unhappy and fearul life beset with a sea of troubles and problems calls for instant thoughtful action. Here's where the Buddha can enlighten man and lead him to the root causes of man's ension and unhappiness, fear and insecurity. For all problems of this would known and unknown, are directly or indirectly related to suffering, *Dukha*.

I do hope that the seventeen research papers by the reputed schalars will be of use to the academicians, scholars and the students.

VISVA-BHARATI

FOUNDED BY

RABINDRANATH TAGORE

ACHARYA
INDER KUMAR GUJARAL
UPACHARYA
DILIP KUMAR SINHA

SANTINIKETAN—731 235
WEST BENGAL, INDIA

Prologue

The Department of Indo-Tibetan Studies at Visva-Bharati, Santiniketan, is a centre for studies and research in Indology in general and Buddhism in particular. In fact, this Department is the first of its kind to introduce Area Study in the University system under the able guidance of Dr. Prabodh Chandra Bagchi. The Department publishes regularly research works on various subjects related and relevant to Indo-Tibetan Studies. I am greatly pleased to mention that Kaveri Books is publishing the fourth volume of the Indo-Tibetan Studies series which I hope will be useful both to the academicians, scholars and students.

Narendra K. Dash

Department of Indo-Tibetan Studies

Contents

Preface *v*

Prologue *vi*

1. Concept of Suffering in Buddhism
   — *Swami Prabhananda* 1

2. Buddhism on Momentariness and Suffering
   — *J.L. Shaw* 6

3. Suffering as Expounded by early Disciple of Buddha
   — *Meena V. Talim* 25

4. Vedanta and Buddhism
   — *C.L.Prabhakar* 39

5. Treatment of Suffering in Gautama's Nyāyasūtra 47
   — *Mrinal Kanti Gangopadhyay*

6. Dukkham Aryasaccam as Depicted in
   The Buddhist Nikaya and Agamas
   — *S.K. Pathak* 54

7. Some Problems Concerning Duhkhasatya
   — *Prabal Kumar Sen* 69

8. Suffering : An Analytical Study
   — *Pradyumna Dube* 85

9. Buddha's Altruism
— *Angraj Chaudhary* 93

10. Concept of Suffering from the Bodhisattva Viewpoint of Self-Dedication
— *J. Sitaramamma* 100

11. Concept of Dukkha in Buddhist and Jain Traditions
— *Bhagchandra Jain* 112

12. Aspects of the Buddhist Social Philosophy-I Understanding Pañcaśīla
— *Dilip Kumar Mohanta* 123

13. Concept of Suffering in Early Buddhism
— *Bimalendra Kumar* 134

14. Buddhism has Solutions from Suffering
— *Bela Bhattacharya* 142

15. Buddhist View of Suffering as discussed in *Abhidharmakośa* of Vasubandhu in *Sarvāstivāda* School
— *Narendra Kumar Dash* 147

16. Suffering as Expounded by Early Disciples of Buddha
—*Dr. Meena V. Talim* 157

17. The Concept of *Dukkha* in the Buddhist *Nikāyas*
— *Dr. (Mrs.) Parineeta Deshpande* 172

Contributors 178

Concept of Suffering in Buddhism

1

Swami Prabhananda

(Namo Bhagavatah Samma-sambudhasya)

The Golden Jubilee Celebration of the Department of Indo-Tibetan Studiės, Visva Bharati, Shantiniketan is an occasion worth-remembering. It brings to our memory the role of three Indian scholars viz. Santarakshita, Padmasambhava and Kamasila, the valuable patronage of Kaviguru Rabindranath Tagore, the contribution of Sylvan Levi, Pandit Bishusekhar Sastri, Probodh Bagchi and others. We all feel proud of the great achievements of this department.

One may justifiably question if there is any need in discussing a topic like the 'concept of suffering' in today's burgeoning liberal society with a market economy and a market-place pragmatics of quick returns and ever-shrinking commitment to a value-system, which have created a tempting euphoria for a merry-making life style. However, to be honest, man was never before in greater need of understanding his problem of suffering as it is today. In spite of the marvellous achievements in science and technology man is more in search of security and happiness, freedom from fear and tensions than ever before. The various problems man is beset with boil down to one problem, which the Buddha called *dukkha* (suffering). He discovered that their cause is *avijja*, ignorance and *tanha*, selfish desire or craving. These are behind lust, hatred and delusion (lobha, dasa, moha) directly responsible for various kinds of individual and social ills including fundamentalism, terrorism and colonisation of different forms. Nevertheless, the Buddha assured that man can overcome his lust to conquer and possess, his thirst for fame, power and domination, his unquenchable desire for selfish ends. Man has potential for the same. The Buddha showed the path, the path to freedom and emancipation.

The concept of *dukkha* (suffering) is the keynote in Buddhist thought. In the early Buddhist scriptures, the word *dukkha* has been used in more than one sense. *Dukkha* is suffering, conflict, unsatisfactoriness in life.It is used in the psychological, physical and philosophical sense according to the context. That it is essential to know, *dukkha* is seen in these words of the Buddha : 'He who sees suffering, sees also the arising of suffering, the cessation of suffering and the path leading to the cessation of suffering'. (Sammohavinodani, 437) All these truths are interconnected and interdependent. This document contains the four noble truths of Gotama Buddha :(a) the world is full of suffering (dukha); (b) the cause of such suffering or pain (dukha-samudaya); (c) the cessation of suffering (dukha-nirodha-gamini-pratipat). All the later Buddhist thoughts, interpretations and several schools of philosophy originated from these four noble truths (arya-satya).

To appreciate Gotama Buddha's radical approach let us remember in brief the historical backdrop of his time. The sacrifices and rituals of the Vedas dominated the socio-religious climate. Simultaneoulsy, however, a belief in the Upanishadic Absolute (Atman or Brahman) had gained strong ground.Side by side, materialistic philosophy had manifested itself in several forms. Of them, one group held the view that all objects come forth of their own accord and by their own nature *(svabhava)*; another group opined that everything is left to destiny *(ajivakas)* and still another group asserted that every perceptible object, including consciousness, is a product of matter-combinations (Charvaka). In this situation, Jainism offered a partial solution by propounding the metaphysical doctrine called *anekantavada* (philosophy of the several), taking into account all the different aspects of the Reality. This was soon over-shadowed by Buddha's philosophy according to which the Reality is neither being nor non-being, but 'becoming'. 'Becoming' is the only truth. This radical humanist philosophy became popular very soon. Buddhism absorbed many new ideas which led to a re-interpratation of the original doctrines and it culminated in major differences of opinion. The Buddhists were split into two main sects.

On a full-moon day of May,578 BC. at the age of thirty five, Gotama Budhisattva comprehended in all their fullness the four noble Truths, and attained enlightenment and became the Buddha. Soon thereafter he walked some 150 miles to Sarnath. He preached before the five ascetics who were struggling with the rigours of extreme asceticism. He advised them to shun both sensual indulgence and self-mortification and recommended the middle path. It is the noble eightfold path, namely, right understanding, right thought, right speech, right action, right livelihood, right effort, right mindfulness and right concentration. This leads a practitioner to the enlightenment, Nibbana or Vimukti. This path, which is, in fact, Buddhism in practice, can be arranged into three groups : Virtue, concentration and wisdom. They constitute the threefold training (tividha-sikkha). Virtue or disciplined behaviour strengthens meditation, meditation promotes wisdom, and wisdom helps one to get rid of the clouded view of things to see life as it really is.

The Buddha's philosophy, in essence, was apparently very simple. It may be summed up in three words: anatman, anitya and duhkha. The notion of Atman is a mere convention. Except nirvana, which is uncompounded (asamskrta), all things are evanescent (anitya), and so are painful (duhkha) and devoid of any everlasting substance.

The Buddha says : duhkkhe loko patitthito (Samyatta-nikaya, I.P 40). It means the world is established on suffering, is founded on suffering. He has elaborated further, 'Birth is suffering, old age is suffering, disease is suffering, death is suffering, sorrow, distress, worry, hankering are suffering; to be united to the disliked is suffering; to be separated from the liked is suffering; not to get what one desires is suffering. In a word the five skandhas are suffering'. (Maha Satipatansakta, 22/8) [H/p.63].

The Buddha's teaching may not immediately touch the heart of many today. But to every sensible person who has trained himself to look at things objectively, it becomes abundantantly clear that suffering is a problem common to all sensate beings. Even if we admit the relative nature of the intensity of suffering, who can deny its pinch ? All other problems known and unknown are directly or indirectly related to suffering.

This single universal problem has different facets; there are economic, social, political, psychological and even religious problems. Solving a problem implies reducing the unsatisfactoriness. Like rheumatism, suffering physical or psychological disappears only to reappear in other forms after sometime. The cause is often not external but subjective in origin.

Some scholars, particularly of the West, have alleged that Gotam Buddha was a pessimist. While Dr. S. Radhakrishnan observed, 'In the whole history of thought no one has painted the misery of human existence in blacker colours and with more feeling than Buddha', he was careful to point out that Buddhism was not pessimistic in outlook. To make people long for escape from this worldliness, the blackness of the world has been a little overdrawn.

Rabindranath Tagore explained the Buddha's standpoint in the following words, 'No religion whatsoever can for a moment stand on the basis of negation. It must have some great truth in its heart which is positive and eternal, and for whose sake Man can offer all that he has, and be glad. And, in this, Buddhism must have its inherent relation and resemblance to that spiritual endeavour in ancient India which led men to leave aside their material possessions and seek the fulfilment of their life.' (The English Writings of Rabindranath Tagore, Vol.III,p.491).

Besides, if Buddhism is painted as pessimistic, then each of the six theistic philosophies i.e. Purva Mimansa, Uttara Mimansa, Nyaya, Vaishesika, Sankhya and Patanjala, share the same blame, for the basic scriptures of most of these philosophies have begun with a chapter on suffering. Like all these philosophies the Buddha does not preach the worthlessness of life or resignations to an inevitable doom. He calls us to revolt against evil and attain a life of nobler qualities, an arhat state.

Here we may profitably recall Swami Vivkananda's distinct view. He considered the Buddha a rebel child of Hinduism; 'The Buddha', he said, 'came not to destroy, but he was the fulfilment, the logical conclusion, the logical development of the religion of the Hindus.' At the Chicago World Parliament of Religions, 1893, the Swami paid high tribite to the Buddha's 'reforming zeal, the wonderful sympathy and charity for everybody and the wonderful leaven which Buddhism had brought to the masses.'

All along these 2500 years the Buddha's noble Eightfold paths beckoned the weary pilgrims to the golden gate of security and peace. Rooted in the Buddha's concept of *dukkha*, the noble eightfold path moistened by *metta* and karuna (love and compassion) assures all men and women irrspective of caste, creed, financial status, learning, etc., of a bright future.

Buddhism on Momentariness and Suffering

2

J.L. Shaw

The aim of this paper is to discuss the Buddhist conception of momentariness and suffering: It is claimed that the Buddhist Philosophers have asserted the equivalence between the following propositions:

a) Everything is momentary

b) Everything is suffering

c) Everything is unique

d) Everything is void

In this paper I shall discuss the nature of the first two propositions and how they are related to nirvana. I shall try to establish the thesis that the proposition 'everything is momentary' is descriptive but the proposition 'everything is suffering' is prescriptive. Hence there are both descriptive and prescriptive propositions in the metaphysics of Buddhism. Thereby some of the objections raised by contemporary interpreters can also be answered.

I

In this section I shall try to establish the view that 'everything is momentary'. The proof of the Buddhist Philosopher is *reductio ad absurdum* argument. Hence I shall refute the view that there are things which are not momentary by demonstrating absurd consequences from this proposition. It is to be noted that the Buddhist Philosophers would assert the equivalence between the following propositions :

1) x is a cause (*kārana*)

2) x is an event (*kādācitka*)

3) x is an agent for an action or result (*arthakriyākarī*)

4) x is real or x exists (*sat*)

5) x is momentary (*kṣaṇika*)

Hence the terms 'karana', 'kadacitka', 'arthakriyakari', 'sat', and 'ksanika' are coextensive. In other words, they would refer to the same thing. Since 'reality' or 'existence' is defined in terms of 'being the agent for an action or result', these two terms would be synonymous. Since an event is something which occurs, it would be an existent entity. Hence it would also be an agent for an action or result. Again, an existent entity is an occurrent phenomenon. Hence it would be an event. The word 'causality' is to be defined in terms of 'the property of being always immediately prior ('*niyata avyavahita* pūrvavartitva') to the effect'. If *a* is the cause of *b*, then *a* is always immediately prior to *b*. It is to be noted that this definition does not require the repeated occurrence of *a* or *b*. Hence it can be explained in terms of the counterfactual proposition 'If *a* would have occurred again, then *b* would have also occurred'. Moreover, there is no plurality of causation. Hence if *a* is the cause of *b,* then *b* is due to *a* and it cannot be without *a*[2]. The word 'momentariness' is defined in terms of 'the property of ceasing to exist after origination'. In other words, if a thing is momentary, then it has no duration. It has only origination and cessation. Hence it has the property of being the counterpositive (negatum) of the no-more type of absence which occurs at the second moment (*dvitiya ksanavrttidhvamsa pratiyogitva*). In favour of the theses 'whatever exists has causal efficacy (arthakriyakaritva)' and 'whatever has causal efficacy is momentary' the Buddhist philosophers have cited examples such as rain-bearing clouds (jaladharapatala). The rain— bearing clouds have causal efficacy as they produce rain.

Moreover, since they do not have duration, they are momentary. Now the Buddhist philosophers try to prove that what holds good of rain—bearing clouds holds good of everything. The proof takes the form of a *reductio ad absurdum*. In other words, the denial of the thesis that everything is momentary will lead to absurdity. Hence the view that a thing has causal efficacy but is not momentary is not tenable.

Now let us consider the refutation of the popular view that there are things which have causal efficacies but are not momentary. This view can take three forms. Suppose *x, y,* and *z* are existent objects; *F*, *G*, and *H* are effects (results of actions); t_1, t_2 and t_3 are past, present and future respectively, or three time-segments. There are three alternatives if a thing is not momentary :

(1) x exists at t_1, t_2 and t_3; but produces the same effect, say F, at t_1, t_2 and t_3.

(2) y exists at t_1, t_2 and t_3. It produces something, say F at t_1, but nothing at t_2 or t_3.

(3) z exists at t_1, t_2 and t_3; but produces different things at different times. Suppose z produces F at t_1, G at t_2 and H at t_3.

The Buddhists would reject the first alternative on the ground that nothing can be repeated. In other words, if x produces F at t_1, then it cannot produce the same effect at t_2 or t_3. This is acceptable to both the proponents and opponents of the view that everything is momentary.

As regards the second alternative, it is said that if y does not produce anything at t_2 or t_3, then it becomes unreal at that time. Since reality is defined in terms of the property of being the agent for an action or result, y would be unreal at t_2 or t_3. In other words, the Buddhists claim that a real object cannot be distinguished from an unreal object if it (real object) does not produce anything. For this reason y would lack existence at t_2 or t_3. Hence this alternative is to be rejected.

In this context it is to be noted that an unreal object such as the golden mountain does not produce anything, but the thought of it may produce an effect such as the desire for it. Hence we should not confuse an unreal object with the thought of it. This argument deals with unreal objects, not with their thoughts. Hence the objection that the thought of an unreal object produces something is wide of the mark.

With respect to the third alternative the Buddhists would ask whether z has the ability (*samarthya*) to produce G or H at t_1.

(a) If it does not have the ability to produce G at t_1, then the question would be how to explain the production of G at t_2. Similarly, the question would be how to explain the production of H at t_3.

In reply, it may be said that z produces G when the auxiliary causal conditions are present. Suppose z produces G at t_2 in conjunction with the auxiliary cause (*sahakarikarana*). Now the question is whether the auxiliary causal condition does something to z or not. If it does something to z, then it produces some effect in z, say n. This n produces G, not z. If the auxiliary causal condition does nothing to z, then it becomes superfluous. If it is said that x and m together produce G, then the collection (samagri) or the coming together is the cause of G, not z. Hence this alternative is not tenable.

(b) If z does have the ability to produce G at t_1, then the question would be whether this ability is explicit or implicit.

(c) If the ability (samarthya) to produce G at t_1 is explicitly present in z and it does not require anything else for its production but does not produce G at t_1, then there would be a contradiction. In other words, z does not produce G at t_1, although it has the explicit ability to produce G at t_1 without any auxiliary causal condition.

(d) In order to avoid the contradiction if it is said that z requires something else, say p, to produce G although the ability is explicitly present, then the previous objections would arise. In other words, the auxiliary causal condition produces something in z, say q, which produces G at t_2. Hence z is not the cause. If z and p together produce G at t_2, then the collection (samagri) becomes the cause, not z.

(e) In order to avoid the above objections it may be suggested that the ability (samarthya) to produce G at t_2 is implicitly present in z at t_1. Similarly, the ability to produce H at t_3 is implicitly present in z at t_1 and t_2. When the auxiliary causal condition, say *r*, is present, the implicit ability becomes explicit and the effect G is produced at t_2. Now the question is whether z is to be identified with this ability.

(f) If it is identified with this ability, then it is not the same z which produces F at t_1. Hence we cannot say that z produces F at t_1 and G at t_2.

(g) If z is not identified with this ability, then the ability which is manifested by r produces the effect G at t_2. Therefore, z does not produce G at t_2. If it is claimed that z in conjunction with the manifestation of the ability produces G at t_2, then the collection (samagri) is to be considered as the cause, not z. This is how the Buddhist philosophers would reject the third alternative which supports the view that a thing which has causal efficacy need not be momentary. Since all the three possible alternatives are untenable, the Buddhists claim that if a thing has causal efficacy, then it is momentary.

From the above discussion it follows that the Buddhist philosophers have tried to establish the thesis that everything is momentary by refuting the thesis that a thing has duration in addition to origination and cessation. Now let us consider the nature of the proposition that everything is momentary. With respect to this proposition, we may ask whether it is analytic, *a priori* or descriptive.

If by 'analytic' we mean the predicate is part of the subject or the predicate concept is contained in the subject concept, then this proposition cannot be treated as analytic. This is due to the fact that the meaning of the word 'thing' does not include the meaning of the word 'momentary'. Hence this proposition is synthetic, not analytic.

Moreover, this proposition cannot be treated as *a priori* if by the word 'a *priori*' we mean not derivable from experience or being independent of experience. This is due to the fact that we learn from experience that a thing ceases to exist after its origination. Hence this proposition is not only synthetic but also *a posteriori*. Now the question is whether it is descriptive or prescriptive. Since the Buddhist philosophers have supported this thesis by refuting the contradictory thesis that there are non-momentary objects, this proposition is descriptive in nature. It is a descriptive metaphysical proposition as it describes the ultimate nature of reality. Hence it is to be treated as a synthetic *a posteriori* descriptive metaphysical proposition.

The above arguments of the Buddhists may be represented by the following diagram.

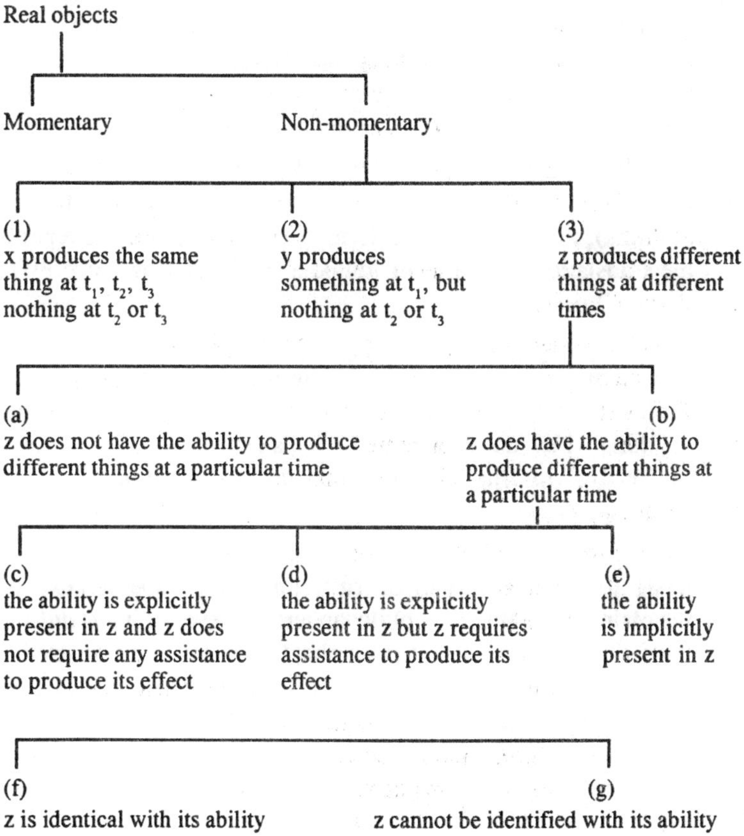

II

In this section I shall discuss in what sense the proposition 'everything is suffering' has been used by the Buddhist philosophers. Let us start with the meaning of the word 'duhkha' and the types of duhkha mentioned by the Buddhist philosophers.

(A) The term 'duḥkha' which is the correlative of 'suhkha' ('happiness') is primarily used to refer to a mental state. It is something which is disliked (hated) for its own sake (svataḥ dveṣ aviṣayaḥ). Hence it is something which is considered as repulsive to all creatures (sarvesāṃ pṛtikūlavedanīyaṃ dukham).[3] It is to be noted that there are two types of 'dveṣa' ('disliking' or 'hatred'). One type of hatred presupposes the knowledge that the thing disliked will lead to greater pain than pleasure. If we know that an action or a thing, say *a*, will lead to greater pain than pleasure, then there is a repulsive attitude towards it. But the hatred towards *duḥkha* does not presuppose any knowledge of this sort. Hence the hatred toward *duḥkha* is spontaneous.[4]

But when the Buddhists claim that everything is suffering (duḥkha), they are using this term in a broader sense. As regards the translation of the term 'duhkha' as 'suffering', Professor Potter Claims:

Duḥkha is often translated as 'pain', 'misery', 'sorrow'— indeed, as used in, e.g., the Buddha's famous sermon on the Four Noble Truths it appears to mean anything unsatisfying or frustrating, anything which does not come to one's expectation. By contrast, 'suffering' in English has connotations of dramatic pain, hardship, *Angst*.[5]

Even if we accept Potter's claim that the word 'duḥkha' is used to signify any unsatisfying or frustrating state, it does not explain the claim of the Buddhist philosophers that everything is *duḥkha* (suffering). This is due to the fact that frustration or dissatisfaction is a state of mind and it is the correlative of satisfaction. Hence, on this view, the word '*duḥkha*' cannot refer to everything. Moreover, 'dissatisfaction' being the correlative of 'satisfaction cannot refer to everything as its meaning depends on there being experiences which are not frustrating. Hence, far from making the claim that everything is *duḥkha*, we cannot even substantiate the view that all life is *duḥkha* or all our experiences are *duḥkha*.

Now let us explain the view of some contemporary interpreters, who have claimed that Buddhism is deeply existentialist. To quote Winston King.[6]:

One has left behind the miasmatic swamps of human passion permeated by an overpowering sense of obscure guilt, where friend and foe can be distinguished only with difficulty, but only to find oneself alone in an infinitely complicated maze in which he, like a lost soul— or lost no-soul— is condemmed to wander endlessly about looking for an exit from this dark and lonely misery but finds none. It is the world of Buddhist dukkha (in Pali, *duhkha*).

It is true that according to Buddhism our life is full of suffering. Birth is suffering, aging is suffering, sickness is suffering, death is suffering. Sorrow, grief, lamentation and despair are suffering. To quote a passage from *The Book of the Kindred Sayings* (*Sanyutta — Nickaya*)[7]:

To be conjoined with things which we dislike: to be separated from the things which we like, - that also in Ill. Not to get what one wants, - that also is Ill. In a word, this body, this fivefold, mass which is based on grasping, - that is Ill.

The Buddhist philosophers have explained an individual or a person in terms of five aggregates (skandhas). Broadly speaking, they are divided into physical form (rūpa) and psychical factors (nāma). The physical form consists of four material elements, namely, earth, water, air and fire. The psychical factors are divided into four types, namely, sensation or feeling (vedana), perception or conception (samjna), mental disposition (saṃskāra) and intellect or consciousness (vijnana). They all are suffering (duḥkha).

Winston King also claimed that the plight of a human being is due to endless repetitious existence. I think he is referring to the 'Wheel of Intervolved Causation' which consists of the following 12 root-causes[8] called 'nidānā':1)Ignorance (avidya), 2) Disposition (saṃskarā), 3) Cognition or consciousness (vijñāna), 4) Name and Form (nama-rupa), 5) Six fields of sense-organs (saḍayatana), 6) Contact (sparśa), 7) Sensation or feeling (vedana), 8) Craving and desire (tṛṣṇa), 9) Attachment (upādāna), 10) Existence or character (bhava), 11) Birth (jati), 12) Old age and death (jarā-maraṇa). Since it is a twelvefold wheel of causation, each of them is caused by its immediate predecessor and is a cause of its immediate successor. According Winston King, there are two types of human predicament. One of them is due to this wheel of causation. We are lost in this wheel having an infinite number of past existences and having the possibility of an infinite number of future existences of the type we are experiencing now or in this life. Another human predicament, according to Winston King, is eternal *aloneness*. Hence the suffering of a human being is due to an eternally individualized repetitious existences. The individualized existence of a human being is suffering and it is interpreted in the same way as an existentialist philosopher would interpret the suffering of a human being. James W. Boyd[9], another contemporary interpreter of Buddhism, has also assigned an existentialist concept of existence to suffering (duḥkha), although he has not claimed that all life is suffering. He claims:

The Buddhist view is not that life is full of suffering, but that the unenlightened life I am living is without real meaning and truth[10].

According to James Boyd, the fundamental concern of the Buddhist philosophers is with human existence, not with the existence of the insentient objects. Hence they are concerned with the meaning of human existence. As regards the relation of a human being to the world, he has assigned the Heideggerian concept of *being—in—a world* to the Buddhist concept of a person. We are already in the world and conditioned by it. The world becomes part and parcel of a human being. A human being is actively engaged in the world. He/she affects the world and is affected by it. This mode of being or human existence is fundamentally misdirected, unenlightened and ill-at-ease. This is what the Buddhist concept of *duḥkha* is, according to James Boyd.

In order to substantiate his claim, he has given a different interpretation to the three types of *duḥkha*. Let us state the Buddhist concept of threefold *duḥkha* as stated in the Pali literature;

a) dukkha dukkha in Pali: It includes ordinary sufferings as well as the fivefold aggregates which constitute an individual. Hence it refers to sufferings due to birth, old age, sickness, death, association with unpleasant things or persons, separation from loved ones and pleasant conditions, not getting what one wants, sorrow, lamentation, pain, grief, and despair. Hence it includes all types of physical and mental suffering[11].

b) Vipariṇāma dukkha: This type of sufferings is due to change. There are times of enjoyment, pleasure or happiness. A happy feeling or condition does not last long. When a feeling of happiness disappears or a happy situation ceases to exist, there is suffering or pain. Hence the experience of disappointment or dissatisfaction is due to change.

c) Saṇkhāra-dukkha: This type of dukkha refers to any type of conditioned states. Since, according to the Buddhist, everything is conditioned, this type of *dukkha* would refer to everything. But James Boyd claims that the word 'saṇkhāra' has two meanings. In one of its uses it refers to dispositional mental states (*sankharakkhanda*), which is one of the five aggregates constitutive of our existence. Another use of it refers to all conditioned things. Hence according to the second usage everything is suffering. But James Boyd claims that the first sense is more important than the second as it deals with human existence. Moreover, he follows the view which claims that the *dukkha* assuaged to the insentient realm is not The Noble Truth of *dukkha*. He says:

'... The Noble Truth of *dukkha* has to do with the sentient realm only, and specifically, with the actual process of my existing (my actions and defilements). The meaning of *dukkha* directly relates to my being-in-the world. When, however, *dukkha* is conceived as a factual claim having to do with a theory of the nature of things— an ontic mode of inquiry— it is not a Noble Truth[12].

The interpretation of James Boyd has several shortcomings:

1) This interpretation would reduce the third type of suffering to the first type as the latter includes the sufferings which are due to five aggregates.

2) Since the Anguttara— nikāya[13] also states that every conditioned entity is impermanent, without self and suffering, the existentialist approach will go against the classical Buddhism.

Hence the interpretation of Winston King would also contradict the claim that everything is suffering. Therefore, neither the thesis that all life is suffering nor the thesis that all unenlightened life is suffering can correctly interpret the view of the Buddhist philosophers that everything is suffering.

(B) Now I would like to explain the claim of the Buddhist philosophers that everything is suffering. It is to be noted that the proposition everything is suffering cannot be expressed by the following symbolic expressions.

a) (x) (If x is an experience of a human being, then x is suffering or produces suffering).

b) (x) (If x is an experience of a sentient being, then x is suffering or leads to suffering).

This is due to the fact that these formulations are confined to the experiences of human beings or sentient beings. Hence the proposition is to be symbolized by the following expression.

c) (x) (x is suffering or leads to suffering).

In order to substantiate this claim we have to prove that pleasant feelings would also lead to suffering. Moreover, we have to establish that insentient objects, such as wind, rocks, distant stars or planets, would also lead to suffering.

It is said in the Sanyutta-Nikāya that pleasant feelings should be regarded as ill. To quote:

"When a brother regards pleasant feelings as ill, painful feelings as a barb, neutral feelings as impermanence, such an one is called, brethren, 'right seeing'"[14].

In support of the claim that pleasant feelings are also suffering it may be said that there is no unmixed or pure happiness. What we call 'pleasure' is saturated with suffering as it is transitory or leads to craving and thereby suffering. Since the union with the loved one does not last long, separation is inevitable. Hence the pleasant feeling due to union with the loved one would also lead to suffering. Similarly, any pleasure due to possession of something would lead to suffering when we lose our possession. Sometimes the thought that we may lose our possession, not the actual loss, produces anxiety and thereby suffering in our life. Hence the so-called pleasant feelings are either momentary or saturated with anxiety, or would lead to pain and suffering. Similarly, the five aggregates which constitute an individual are causally related to pain, sorrow, anxiety or suffering. Hence they are also to be considered as suffering.

As regards insentient phenomena such as wind, rain or rocks, it may be said that they are also causally related to pain or suffering, although they are not pain or suffering if taken in isolation from a sentient being. Since rain causes flood or damages, it is causally related to the sorrows or sufferings of sentient beings. Similarly heat or wind may produce pain or suffering in sentient beings. Hence an inanimate object is also causally related to suffering. The proposition that everything is suffering may be stated in the following way:

d) (x) (x is suffering if x is related to suffering or the feeling of pain by the relation of identity or it is related to suffering or the feeling of pain by causal relation, direct or indirect).

As regards the nature of this proposition, it is to be noted that it is neither analytic nor a *priori*. Hence the meaning of the word 'object' or 'thing' does not contain the concept of suffering. Since the justification put forward in favour of this proposition is empirical, it cannot be claimed to be *a* priori. Hence it is a synthetic *a posteriori* proposition. As regards the nature of the argument, unlike the argument in favour of the view that everything is momentary, supporters of this thesis have not used the *reductio ad absurdum* argument.

The critics of this type of argument would raise the following objections against the thesis that everything is suffering.

1) Even if we claim that wind or rain is causally related to the suffering of a sentient being, we cannot claim that a distant star or planet is similarly related to the pain of a sentient being. This is due to the fact that their signals have not yet affected any sentient being or might not be causally related to any sentient being. Hence the phenomena which are not

causally related to suffering or pain would not come under the range of the values of the variable 'x' in the proposition (d).

2) Even wind or rain cannot be said to cause suffering unconditionally. If there is drought, the rain, far from causing sorrow, will bring the message of hope and happiness. Moreover, the same cold wind which causes suffering to one may cause happiness to another. Hence a phenomenal object is not unconditionally related to suffering or happiness.

3) By using this type of argument one may equally come to the conclusion that everything is happiness. Since our sorrows and sufferings are transitory, they are the passing phases of our life. When suffering ceases to exist, we experience happiness. Hence we can also utter with Shelly, 'If winter comes can spring be far behind?'.

4) Moreover, if it is claimed that *nirvana* is something positive, not simply negative, then it is something which is also outside the range of the values of the variable 'x' in our formulation (d). The state of *nirvana* has been claimed to be beyond death. It is not caused not born, not produced: It is also beyond all becoming[15]. Since the world of being is outside the scope of the quantifier 'all', we have to say that every phenomenal object or thing is suffering, not everything. If suffering is used as a stepping stone to the attainment of *nirvana* which is a state of being and bliss, then suffering, being causally related to something which is not suffering, cannot be contrasted with happiness or bliss. Hence this interpretation of *nirvana* would create more problems than it solves.

From the above discussion it follows that neither the existentialist approach nor the non-existentialist (essentialist) approach to the proposition that everything is suffering is satisfactory. The former ends up with the discussion of human suffering and consequently denies the truth of the proposition that everything is suffering. The latter approach is hard to substantiate, either as a scientific or metaphysical truth. According to our positive thesis both the approaches are unsatisfactory because both of them have taken this proposition as descriptive. The proposition is to be taken as prescriptive or evaluative. For this reason there is no *reductio ad absurdum* proof in favour of this proposition as we have in favour of the proposition that everything is momentary. Since the proposition everything is suffering is not descriptive, it cannot be said to be true or false. Since it is prescriptive[16] in nature, it is prescribed for those who are seekers of truth, knowledge and reality. In other words, it is prescribed for the seekers of liberation, *mokṣa* or *nirvana*. The prescriptive form of this proposition may be stated in the following way:

e) (x) (If x is a seeker of nirvana, then x ought to treat everything as suffering).

This imperative is similar to the Categorical Imperative of Kant if it is stated in the following way:

(x) (If x seeks to realize moral values, then x ought to treat human beings not simply as a means to an end but as an end in itself)[17].

From the above discussion of the nature of the proposition that everything is suffering it follows that it is not on a par with the proposition that everything is momentary. The former is prescriptive in nature, while the latter is descriptive in nature. The former is evaluative as it implies a value judgment, while the latter is not evaluative as it does not imply a value judgment. But both of them are synthetic *a posteriori* propositions.

III

In this concluding section I would like to point out how both the propositions are related to the Buddhist concept of *nirvana (nibbana* in Pali).

It is to be noted that the word 'nirvana' or 'nibbana' has been interpreted in several ways or it has several connotations. It consists of ni+vana (or nir+vaṇa)[18]. The negative particle '*ni*' means absence or cessation and the word '*vana*' means weaving or craving. Hence, the etymological meaning of '*nirvana*' is cessation or extinction of craving. The following three types of craving have been mentioned in the Buddhist literature[19].

1) The craving that motivates physical and vocal actions;
2) The craving that stimulates the imagination or fantasy;
3) The craving which is latent as a disposition.

The first type of craving motivates the transgression of ethical conduct. The second type of craving is a causal condition for the thought (or imagination) of objects which we usually desire. The third type of craving yields the craving for existence. Since '*nirvana*' implies or connotes cessation of craving, it would imply cessation of all the three types of craving. The state of *nirvana* does not imply the extinction or the cessation of the individual, but only the cessation of his/her cravings which are causally related to the defilements of attachment, aversion and delusion. Hence *nirvana* does not imply the total extinction of life, but only extinction of the life of illusion, passion and craving[20]. But some of the Buddhist texts, including *Dhammapada*, have emphasized the positive aspects of the state of nirvana.

To quote Dhammapada:

> Health is the highest gain; contentment is the greatest wealth, trustful are the best kinsmen; *nibbana* is the highest bliss[21].

Even if '*nirvana*' implies a positive state of bliss or peace, or tranquility, there cannot be *nirvana* without the cessation of craving or the extinction of selfish desires or defilements. Hence any interpretation of the word '*nirvana*' would imply the cessation of craving which is one of the links or factors in the 'Wheel of Intervolved Causation'. Since the cessation of one of the links in the wheel of causation would eventually lead to the cessation of the Wheel itself, *nirvana* may be equated with the cessation of the Wheel of Causation. This extended sense also implies something negative which is related to the cessation of craving. Hence the cessation of craving may be taken as the cardinal connotation of the word '*nirvana*'.

The distinctive feature of Buddhism is that both the theses that 'everything is momentary' and that 'everything is suffering' would lead to the cessation of craving, but not in the same way. It is claimed that the unwavering idea' (*vasana*) that all impressions are momentary is the way which will lead us to liberation[22]. Hence the thesis that 'everything is momentary' would lead us to *nirvana* by removing ignorance about the nature of things and thereby craving for things. It is to be noted that due to ignorance about the reality we take things to be permanent or semi-permanent. We cling to the objects of our liking as we take them to be permanent or to have some duration. Since we take the objects to have some duration, we expect the same type of actions or reactions from them over a period of time. We get hurt or frustrated when our expectations are not being fulfilled. But if we realize that things are momentary, then we do not expect the same type of actions or reactions from an object. Moreover, it would pave the way for the feeling of non-attachment as objects cannot remain the same. Hence the doctrine of momentariness by removing the veil of ignorance about the real nature of things would lead us to the cessation of craving.

The thesis that 'everything is suffering' has also been proposed by other schools of Indian philosophy, such as the Yoga system. To an enlightened yogi, according to the yoga system, every object will give rise to suffering[23]. Hence an omniscient yogi will be able to grasp the truth of the proposition that every object can cause suffering or will lead to suffering. But according to the Buddhist philosophers the prescriptive proposition that everything is suffering is used as a means to *nirvana*. If we realize that a thing will cause suffering, then far from having a craving for it, there will be a repulsive feeling against it. When there is a cessation of craving for any object, we realize *nirvana*. It is also claimed that it can be realized here or in this life. So the Buddhist philosophers have used both the propositions for the cultivation of the feeling of detachment (or non-attachment) towards the objects of this world. But the other schools of Indian philosophy have used only the pervasive features of suffering for the cultivation of the feeling of detachment as they have not accepted the thesis that everything is momentary. Moreover, some Buddhist masters have emphasized so much the importance of suffering that it has assumed the status of a guru. To quote Gampopa[24], a Tibetan Mahayana master:

> Sorrow, being the means of convincing one of the needs of the religious life, is a *guru*. Misfortune, being the means of leading one to the Doctrine, is also a *guru*.

Moreover, it is claimed that illness and tribulations are teachers of piety. In other words, sorrows or sufferings help us cultivate moral virtues such as benevolence towards all creation (*maitri*) and compassion towards the distressed (*karuna*). Hence the prescriptive proposition that everything is suffering has a twofold effect on us. The negative effect is the cessation of craving and the positive effect is the promotion of the cultivation of moral virtues. The cultivation of moral virtues will dissolve our ego but the cessation of craving will lead us to the realization of *nirvana*. From the above discussion it follows that both the propositions are related to *nirvana*, but not in the same way.

References

1. sarvam ksanikam ksanikam duhkham duhkham svalaksanam svalksanam sunyam sunyamiti, *Sarvadarsana — samgraha* of Madhavacarya, quoted in panchanan, Bhattacharya's *Bauddhadarsanam*, p 23; see also author's 'Causality: Samkhya, Bauddha and Nyaya, *Journal of Indian Philosophy,* 2002.
2. jasmine sati satutpadyate, jasmine asati jannotpadyate, tat tasya karanasya karyamiti, *op*. cit., p 119.
3. Dinesh Chandra Sastri, *Aspects of Indian Psychology*, p 32.
4. Ibid., p 34.
5. K. Potter, 'Suffering in the Orthodox Philosophical Systems : Is There any ?', in *Suffering* : *Indian Perspectives*, edited by K.N. Tiwari; see also B.K. Matilal's 'On the Universality of Suffering' in *Suffering* : *Indian Perspectives* and 'The Enigmas of Buddhism' in *Language, Logic and Reality.*
6. Winston L. King, *Buddhism and Christianity* : *Some Bridges of Understanding*, p 111; see also David E. Cooper's *Meaning*, ch 7.
7. *The Book of Kindred Sayings (Sanyutta-Nikaya)*, Vol 5, translated by F.L. Woodward, The Pali Text Society, Oxford, 1997, p 357.
8. G. Jha, Tattvasangrah of Santaraksita and kamalasila, Vol 1, Oriental Institute, Baroda, p 1.
9. James W. Boyd, 'Suffering in Teravada Buddhism', in *Suffering*: *Indian Perspectives*, edited by K.N. Tiwari.
10. Ibid., p, 162.
11. Ibid., pp. 154-155; see also *The First Discourse of the Buddha* by Venerable Dr. Rewata Dhamma, pp. 56-57.
12. Ibid., p, 160.
13. *The Book of Kindred Sayings (Sanyutta-Nikaya)*, translated by F.L. Woodward, p. 139.

14. Ibid., p. 139.
15. Encyclopaedia Britannica, Vol 3, 1979, p. 378; see also *Suffering : Indian Perspectives*, p. 165.
16. For more of this topic, see author's 'Empty Terms: The Nyaya and The Buddhists', *Journal of Indian Philosophy*, 1974, and 'The Advaita Vedanta on Meaning', in *Vedanta: Concepts and Application*.
17. I. Kant, *Groundwork of the Metaphysic of Morals*, translated by H J Paton, pp. 95-98.
18. Depak Kumar Barua, 'The Foundations of Living Faiths', in *Faith, Morality & Culture*, edited by U.R. Bhattacharya and H. Bandopadhyay, p. 50; and Monier-Williams, Sanskrit-English Dictionary, p. 557.
19. Rewata Dhamma, *The First Discourse of the Buddha*, p. 87.
20. See also Hajime Nakamura, *A Comparative History of Ideas*, pp. 259-262; and Haridas Bhattacharya, 'Early Buddhism', in *History of Philosophy : Eastern and Western*, edited by S.Radhakrishnan.
21. *The Dhammapada*, translated by Narada Thera, p. 57.
22. Ksanikah, sarvasamskara iti ya vasana sthira sa margah iti vijneyah sa ca moksohbhidhiyate, quoted in *Bauddhadarsanam*, p. 129.
23. *Patanjala Darsana*, translated with commentary by Purna Chandra Sharma, pp 126-127, sutra 2/15; see also *Sankhyakarika*, translated by Purna Chandra Sharma.
24. Quoted in *Suffering : Indian perspectives*, p. 170.

Bibliography

Barua, Dipak Kumar, 'The Foundation of Living Faiths: Buddhisn' in *Faith, Morality and Culture* edited by U.R. Bhattacharyya and H. Bandopadhyay, Sanskrit Pustak Bhaudar, Calcutta, 1996.

Bhattacharya, Haridas, 'The Buddhish Philosophy', in *History of Philosophy: Eastern and Western*, vol. I, (ed.) S. Radhakrishnan, George Allen and Unwin Ltd. London, 1967.

Bhattacharya, Panchanan, *Bauddha-darsanam* of Madhavacarya, translated with commentary, Shibani Bhattacarya Publisher, Calcutta, Bengali year 1401.

Boyd, Jams W., 'Suffering in Theravada Buddhishm', in *Suffering : Indian Perspectives*, edited by K.N. Tiwari, Motilal Banarridas, Delhi 1986.

Cooper, David E., *Meaning*, Acumen, England, 2003-11-112.

Dhamma, Rewata, *The First Discourse of the Buddha*, Wisdom Publications, Boston, 1997.

Encyclopaedia Britannica, Vol. 3, articles on Buddhism, 1979.

First Indian reprint, Cosmo Publications, New Delhi, 1979.

George Allen and Unwin Ltd, London, 1963.

In *Suffering*: *Indian Persepctives*,

Jha, Ganganath, translation of *Tattvasangraha* of Santaraksita and Kamalasila, vol. 1, Oriental Institute, Baroda, 1937.

Kant, I., *Groundwork of the Metaphysic of Morals*, translated by H.J. Paton, Harper Torchbooks, New York, 1956.

King, Winston L., *Buddhism and Christianity*; Some Bridges of Understanding, Madhavacarya, *Sarvadarsan-Samgraha*, translated by E.B. Cowell and A.E. Gough, Matilal, B.K., *Logic, Language and Reality*, Motilal Banarsidass, Delhi, 1990.

Max Muller, F., (ed.) *Buddhist Mahayana Texts*, Sacred Book of the East Series, Motilal Banarsidass, Delhi, 1968.

Max Muller, F., (ed.) *Vinaya Texts*, vol. XLIX, Sacred Book of the East Series, vol. XIII, Motilal Banarsidass, Delhi, 1968.

Monier-Williams, M., *Sanskrit-English Dictionary*, Motilal Banarsidass, Delhi, 1984, p. 557.

Nakamura Hajime, *A Comparative History of Ideas*, Kegan Paul, London, 1986.

Narain, Harsh, 'Suffering in Mahayana Buddhism', in *Suffering* : *Indian Perspectives*, edited by K.N. Tiwari, Motilal Banarsidass, Delhi 1986.

Potter, Karl H., '*Suffering in the Orthodox Philosophical Systems*: *Is There Any* ?', Edited by K.N. Tiwari, Motilal Banarsidass, Delhi 1986.

Sharma, Purna Chandra, *Patanjala-Darsana*, translated with commentary, West Bengal State Book Board, 1983.

Sharma, Purna Chandra, *Samkhyakarika*, translated with commentary, West Bengal State Book Board, 1983.

Shastri, Dinesh Chandra, *Aspects of Indian Psychology*, Ramakrishna Mission Ashrama, West Bengal, 1988.

Shaw, J.L., 'Empty Terms: The Nyaya and the Buddhists', Journal of *Indian Philosophy*, 1974.

Shaw, J.L., 'The Advaita Vedanta on Meaning', in *Vedanta*: *Concepts and Application*, The R.K. Mission Institute of Culture, Calcutta 2000.

Shaw, J.L., 'Causality : Samkhya, Bauddha and Nyaya', *Journal of Indian Philosophy*, 2002.

Thera, Narada, *The Dhammapada*, translated with notes, John Murray, London, 1972.

Woodward, F.K., translation of *Sanyutta-Nakaya* (*The Book of Kindred Sayings*), vols IV and V, The Pali Text Society, Oxford, 1996.

Suffering as Expounded by early Disciple of Buddha

3

Meena V. Talim

In the present paper I have selected some of the verses of monks (Theragāthā) and nuns (Therīgāthā) that would explain their ideas about Dukka- Suffering. The purpose of choosing these two books from Khuddaka Nikaya is to get first hand information about suffering from their autobiographical gāthās. Most of these monks and nuns were contemporary to the Buddha. However Dr. Winternitz has pointed out that these gāthās were not collected and carefully preserved during Gotamas life-time and soberly fixed soon after his death.[1] Therefore they may have been finally fixed between the third century B.C. and 1st century B.C.[2] I have also taken into account another book, namely, "Milind -Pañha' (1st century A.D.) for our study. The purpose of selecting this book is to have a non-canonical book containing a dialogue between a lay-follower and a Buddhist monk. Thus these two different sources perhaps may help us to get a clear picture of the subject.

I

The verses (gāthās) of monks do not relate to our personal 'Dukkha' but they speak about it as the fact of life. They are conscious, watchful and aware of 'Dukkha' which they have, accept it as a universal phenomenon. Most of the monks understand it by carrying on experiments in their lives. Their autobiographical verses, therefore, are instructive and informative. The verses of the following monks will reveal to us their approach to conquer 'Dukkha'.

Kātiyāna Thero[3]

उट्ठेहि निसीद कातियान : मा निद्दाबहुलो अहु, जागरस्सु।
मा तं अलसं पमत्तबन्धु; कूटेने व जिनातु मच्चुराजा।

Get up oh Kātīyāna, do not sit, you have slept for a long time, be awake now. Do not be lazy, oh imprudent monk, you have to win over a bad one, the King of death.

सेय्यथापि महासमुद्दवेगो, एवं जातिजरावत्तते तं।
सो करोहि सुदीपम'त्तनो त्वं, न हि ताणं तव विज्जते अञ्ञे।

A great ocean with torrents of flood engulfs all, similarly birth and old age vanquishes all. Therefore make an island for yourself. There is no other refuge to you than your own conquest.

Nhātakamuni Thero[4]

Monk Nhātakamuni was asked, " You are very weak and feeble, what will you do in this forest?"

He answered:-

पितिसुखेन विपुलेन फरित्वान समुस्सयं।
लूखाम्पि अभिसम्भोन्तो विहारिस्सामि कानने।।
भावेन्तो सत्त बोज्झङ्गे, इन्द्रियानि बलानि च।
झानसुखमसम्पन्नो विहिरिस्सामं कानने।

Though I am weak, I shall wander fearlessly in this forest, spreading everywhere the happiness of love (Mettā). I shall cultivate seven factors of wisdom that will strengthen my organs of senses. I shall wander in the forest enjoying the bliss of meditation. This monk though weak in physic is strong in mind. His confidence overwhelms through his diction, as if he has found the key to get rid of his sorrow.

Upasena Vangantoputto Thero[5]. The monk says the following gathas:-

न सो उपवदे कञ्चि उपघातं विवज्जये।
संवुतो पातिमोक्खास्मिं मतञ्ञू च 'स्स' भोजने।।
सुग्गहितनिमित्तस्स चित्तस्सु प्पादककोविदो।
समथं अनुयुञ्जेय्य कालेन च विपस्सनं।।

Do not retaliate or hurt anyone by speech.

Be restrainful, follow the rules of Patimokkha, be moderate in food.

Stick to good objects of meditation, control your mind and be master of your mind,

Follow Samatha and gradually shift to Vipassanā.

One can note here that monk Upasena begins his experiment by being restrainful to speech and food, then concentrates on the preliminary stage of meditation, namely, Samatha and finally diverts himself to Vipassanā. These experimental stages that begin from observing disciplinary rules to cultivate Vipassanā are positive ways to overcome 'Dukkha'.

Sāriputta Thero[6]

Monk Sāriputta said:-

'ना' भिनन्दामि मरणं ना' भिन्दामि जीवितं।
कालञ्ञ पटिकङ्खामि निब्बिसं भतको यथा।।
उभयेन इदं मरणे 'व ना' मरणं पच्छा वा पुरे वा।
पटिपङ्कथ मा विनस्सथ, खणो मा उपच्चगा।।

I do not enjoy death nor do I enjoy life,

I think of time just as a labourer on wages craves for boiled rice.

I have discarded (the thoughts) of both, namely death or no death (life),

Whether at early (young) age or later age (old age).

Do not destroy time, let not even a moment go wasted. Here monk Sāriputta gives importance to the time factor and warns not to be emotional as regards life or death but to make use of every moment of life, to get rid of Dukkha.'

Tālapuṭo Thero[7]

दुक्ख' ति खन्धे पटिपस्स योनिसो।
यतो च दुक्खं समुदेति तं जहं।।
इधे' दुक्खस्स करोहि अन्तं।
इतिं स्सु मं चित्त पुरे नियुञ्जसि।।

Dukkha means five elements that give rise to birth.

Discard those that cause Dukkha.

End your Dukkha here only (in this life)

This is what my mind had decided, a long time ago.

Here the monk give more stress on the five senses (Pañca Khandhani) and narrates his Personal experience that the control over mind will help to end dukkha.

Pārāpāriya Thero[8]

Here the monk says:-

इन्द्रियानि मनुस्सानं हिताय' हिताय च।
अरक्खितानि अहिताय रक्खितानि हिताय च।
मनं चे'तेहि धम्मेहि यो न सक्कोति रक्खितुं।
ततो दुकखम'न्वेति सन्नेहे' तेहि पञ्चाहि।।

Man's organs of senses (five) are meant for his benefit and loss. When not controlled, they lead one to loss but when controlled lead one to benefit. All worldly phenomena arise through one's mind which one cannot control. Thereby one suffers and all these arise through five (senses). Here the monk does not blame the sensory elements of human beings but shows their positive side. He argues that the mind of man plays a key role to control the sensory elements, eventually to end Dukkha.

Aññākoṇḍañño Thero[9] said:-

रजं ऊहतञ्च वातेन यथा मेधो पसामये।

एवं सम्मन्ति सङ्कप्पा यदा पञ्ञाय पस्सति।।
सब्बे सङ्खारा अनिच्चा'ति यदा पञ्ञाय पस्सति।।
अथ निब्बिन्दति दुकखे, एस भग्गे विसुद्धिया।।

Just as the wind blows away dust or disperses clouds, similarly when one sees with wisdom, all thoughts vanish away. When one realizes through wisdom that all component things are impermanent, then suffering will be quenched; this is a path of purity.

Here the monk gives more importance to wisdom and instructs that the whole process of getting rid of Dukkha is based on it.

II

In Therigāthā nuns reveal to us different layers of mundane suffering. A nun's approach is simple, innocent but touching, mainly related to womanhood. Kisāgotami loses her only child and runs from door to door to get a few mustard seeds to revive her child. She talks about the pains and agony of giving birth to a child. Vaḍḍhamātā, an aged mother, speaks about, the Dukkha of a woman who loved and looked after her children who have discarded her in her old age. Isidāsi tells us about the sad experiences of her married life who was married thrice. She does everything for them, lives with her husband as a dāsi would do; inspite of such humiliations her marriages were broken. Ambāpāli, the courtesan of Vesali, realizes the transitory elements of body, but her agony is no less, Chāpā, the rustic, mischievous and jolly girl is not able to understand her husband, on intellectual level. Bhaddākuṇḍalakesā is young and innocent, whose love is trampled on by her wicked and shrewd husband. Patācārā,the daughter of a rich merchant, elopes with a servant of the house and suffers throughout her life. All these nuns talk about their sad experiences and mentioned them as darts of sorrow that had pierced their heart.*

One cannot discard these feminine experiences as personal but these are the facts of a woman's sufferings. In modern generation too one can find many women suffering in more or less similar situations. This means that the category of woman's Dukkha is different and is

* अब्बुहि वत मे सल्लं दुछसं हदयनिस्सितं।

more related to their psychological factors. However, through her ego-centric Dukkha she focuses on a broader universal Dukkha. Her intensity of personal sorrow makes her more analytical in expounding the norms of the Buddha. She is perceptible to the three teachings of the Buddha namely Dukha, anattā and anīccatā.

The nuns have understood the solution to the Dukka that the Buddha had meant. Their ways of handling Dukkha are different from those of the monks. Most of these nuns speak of different procedures that they have followed. Some say that, "I went into seclusion."[10] Some say that "they meditated at night- 'In the first watch of the night I have remembered my previous births, in the second watch of the night divine eye was washed and in the third watch of the night an entire darkness of sensory elements vanished away".[11] Some like Patācārā said, "I entered into the vihāra holding a lamp in the hand, there I sat, cleaned the wick and concentrated on the lamp; my mind became free and obtained nibbāna.[12] Mahāpajāpati Gotamī said, 'I have followed the Eight-fold noble Path and realised the cessation of suffering.[13]

Let us study some verses of the nuns:-

Sāmā and Abhayā Theri said:-

बहूहि दुक्खधम्मेहि अप्पमादरताय मे।
तण्हकखयो अनुप्पत्तो कतं बुद्धस्स सासनं।।[14]

I have been very watchful over the constituents of Dukkha;

I have obtained cessation of craving by following the teachings of the Buddha.

Sujātā Theri said:[15]

सुत्वा च महेसिस्स सच्चं सम्पटिविज्झ' हं।
तत्थेव विरजं धम्मं फुर्सायं अमतं पदं।।
ततो विञ्ञातसद्धम्मा पब्बजिं अनगारियं।
तिस्सो विज्ञा अनुप्पत्ता अमोधं बुद्धसासनं।।

I have followed the four noble truths, after hearing the great Sage,

There only I touched the peerless norm and have obtained the state of nectar.

Then, after knowing the good law, I have renounced the world, I followed the teaching of the wise one and obtained three kinds of knowledge.

Mahāpajāpati Gotami Theri[16] recited the following verse:-

सब्बदुक्खं परिञ्ञातं हेतु तण्हा विसोसिता।
अरियट्ठङ्गिको मग्गो निरोधो फुसितो मया।।

I have very well understood Dukkha and its cause; thereby my cravings have been dried up.

I have obtained the path of cessation by following the eight-fold noble path.

Guttā Theri[17] the nun said:-

रागं मानं अविज्जञ्च उद्धच्चञ्च विवज्जिय।
संयोजनानि छेत्वान दुकखस्स' नां करिस्ससि।।

I have discarded lust, pride, and ignorance, and by the cutting of all these bondages one can end Dukkha.

Kisāgotami Theri[18]

भावितो मे मग्गे अरियो अट्ठङ्गिको अमतगमि।
निब्बाणं सच्छिकतं धम्मादासं अपोक्खि' हं।।
अहम'म्हि कन्तसल्ला ओहितभारा कतं मे कारणीयं।
किसागोतमी थेरी सुविमुत्तचित्ता इमं भणी 'ति।।

I have cultivated the noble eight-fold path that leads to immortality.

I have witnessed Nibbāṇa and seen clearly the Dhamma as one would see oneself in the mirror.

I have taken out the dart (that had pierced my heart), the burden has been removed; I have done whatever was necessary.

Nun Kisāgotami says this, whose mind has been emancipated.

Rohiṇi Theri[19] says:-

सचे भायसि दुकखस्स सचे ते दुक्खमप्पियं।
उपेहि ब्रुद्धं सरण धम्मं सङ्ञ्च तादिनं।
समादियाहि सीलानि तं ते अत्थाय हेहिति।।

If you are afraid of Dukkha, if you dislike Dukkha, then take refuge in Buddha, Dhamma and Samgha; observe the moral precepts which will benefit you.

This is a direct appeal to those who want to overcome Dukkha. She advises them to follow the moral precepts.

Sihā Theri[20] :

She was a niece of Sinhā Senāpati. She had renounced the world but was unable to control her mind for seven years.

ततो रज्जुं गहेत्वान पाविसिं वनमन्तरं।
वरं मे इध उब्बन्धं यञ्च हीनं पुना चरे।।
उळहं पासं करित्वान रुकखसाखाय बन्धिय।
पाक्खिपिं पासं करित्वान रुकखसाखाय बन्धिय।
पक्खिपिं पासं गीवाय अथ चित्तं विमुन्नि मे।।

I entered a thicket of the forest, taking a rope with me.

It is better if I tie myself here than to lead a low life.

I fastened the noose to the branch of a tree.

I kept my neck in the noose and that very moment my mind was enlightened.

Here one can see that a frustrated nun had tried to commit suicide. But her desire to get control of her mind is so earnest and intense that ultimately emancipation dawns upon her. Perhaps this example may have given solace to others.

Thus we observe that a nun initially looks at Dukkha as a calamity. She is shattered, depressed and disgusted at the routines of life. But she makes a desperate, earnest and honest attempt to come out of Dukkha and she overpowers Dukkḥa, ultimately. There is more of obedience in her attitude. She follows the eight-fold noble path, does meditation and achieves spiritual state. From her egocentric sorrow she realizes universal Dukkha.

A monk on the other hand looks at suffering as a challenge. He is more cool; he has nothing to grumble about his paṣt life. He is more attentive to Dukkha. He analytically studies the four noble truths. He critically ensures his path through meditative means. He enjoys freedom more deligently and volunteers to help his brethren.

However, one can notice a common element in both the communities. There is no morose or sinking attitude in accepting the sorrow. Both accept it as a reality of life and face it boldly. There is no despair or pessimism of any sort. Their *modus operandi* is the same. Both rigorously follow meditative courses, namely, Samatha and Vipassanā. They also recommend these two forms of meditation as the keys that would relieve one from Dukkha. There is more of positive and optimistic thought in their thinking. Dukkha becomes a starting point to obtain enlightenment.

III

King Menandros or Milinda of Sagala has his roots in Greece (215-90 B.C.). A foreigner by birth but a true, faithful disciple of Buddha, he was a philosopher and great exponent of the Buddha's doctrine. His dialogues with monk Nāgasena reveal a touch of Greek (Plato) style. The debate consists of inferences, anologies, and syllogistic reasoning. One can notice the approach and attitude of Milinda-pañha different from those in the books of Khuddaka-nikāya. Both were written on different levels. We must remember the gāthās of monks and nuns are entirely devoted to Buddha's faith and teaching and, in the case of King Milinda, he is a wise householder, possessing a kingdom. He does not take anything for granted as a monk or a nun would do. He is more discerning and truthful. He first makes a proposition, followed by argument to find out the *pros* and *cons* of the point. This is a very different and interesting approach than that of Thera and Theri gāthās.

The questions about Dukkha were asked by King Milinda,. These I find very interesting, appealing and erudite. The scope of the subject becomes two fold as it *pertains to a householder and recluse*. The attitude of the former is worldly, mundane and the latter is more philosophical and missionary. Both participants are proficient and therefore the dialogue becomes interesting and impressive. Now, let us examine some of the questions.

In Milindapañho, wisdom (Pañña) is considered as a basic factor to realize and get rid of Dukkha. Therefore a question was asked "What are the characteristics of wisdom? (भन्ते नागसेन, किं लकखवणा पञ्ञा?). Monk Nagasena answered, "Wisdom is one that cuts (छेदनं), that which enlightens (ओभासनं). After the rise of wisdom (पञ्ञा) one can dispel the darkness of ignorance and realize the four noble truths which lead a monk to see the end of Dukkha, anicca and anatta."-21

In other words, it means to understand अरियसच्चानि that wisdom is very necessary, without which one cannot end the Dukkha. A simile given in this context says that just as a lamp when taken into a house which is dark, dispels the darkness and everything is made clear, similarly the darkness caused by ignorance vanishes with the help of wisdom.

The next question was, "Oh Rev. one, where does the पञ्चा go ?'[22] The Monk answered, "Wisdom (पञ्चा), after giving rise to good act, vanishes but the realization of suffering and the end of suffering, impermanence and anātta do not vanish.

Here is a smile : just as a certain man, at night calls a writer to write by lighting a lamp and when the writing is complete the lamp is extinguished but the writing remains similarly पञ्ञा vanishes but not the realization of दु:क्ख.

Another simile is: a physician makes a medicine from five roots and cures the patient. Once when the patient is cured there is no need of the medicine. Similarly पञ्ञा brings under control all the five sense organs along with their defilements (किलेसा ऽ). After this act (पञ्ञा) there is no need of पञ्ञा.

King Milinda asked, "Oh Rev., one calms oneself. How come one feels a pain of Dukkha ?[23] (भन्ते नागसेन, यो न पटिसन्दति, वेदेति सो किंञ्चि दुक्खं वेदनं'न्ति।) The answer is, "Yes, sometimes he does and sometimes he does not," and the explanation is, "He experiences physical pain (कायिक वेदनं) but not mental pain (चेतसिक वेदनं)". Again a question was asked, "How is it that such a calm one does experience the pain of Dukkha? Can he not pacify it ?" The answer is ,"No, oh King, for Arahat does not have repulsive or courteous feeling for pain. He does not allow unripe pain to fall down nor does he welcome that pain which is mature".

In short, Arhat is indifferent to pain and therefore he is indifferent to Dukkha. He allows (physical) pain to take its own course. Thus Arhat is not totally free from कायिकदुक्खं. The greatest example cited is that of the Buddha who in his last days suffered from dysentery.

King Milinda asked another tricky Question, "Oh Rev Nagasena, is good feeling सुखावेदना कुसला वा अकुसला वा अब्याकता? [24] meritorious or demeritorius or indifferent?" The answer is, "It can be all three". Again King said, "If that is so, if merit does not give Dukkha, if Dukkha is not merit then why not merit (कुसल) end Dukkha and not give rise to Dukkha ?"

The answer is given in a simile. "If in one hand of a man a hot-iron ball is kept and in another hand an ice-ball is kept, then will not that man burn both his hands? "Yes, he will."

"This means that both hot and cold objects can burn the hand; they cannot stop the pain. Similarly कुसल and अकुसल can cause pain दुक्ख."

King Milinda asked, "Do you exert (वायाम) force to get rid of the Dukkha of the past ? Or future ? or present ?"[25] Rev. Nagasena said", "No, Oh king". "If that is so then why do you exert yourself ". "Oh King I exert so that suffering should vanish and other Dukkha will not rise; for this purpose I exert myself".

Again the king had questioned him, "Do you think that you would have Dukkha in future(अनागत दुक्खं)?" The monk said, "No,

Sire'. "Then why do you exert for अनागत दुक्खं, which would not be there ?", The monk gave similies:-

"Oh King, is there a possibility of your enemy who has been defeated by you, to wage war against you?" "Yes". "Then do you prepare yourself after his attack ?". "No, we make preparations regularly including regular parades of elephants, horses, chariots, army, etc., and this we do to avoid future dangers". "Oh King, just as you prepare yourself to face danger which is not there, similarly we monks exert ourselves". The monk gave other similies. "Just as one does not start digging a well when he is thirsty but digs it for his future provision. Or just as a man does not start ploughing his field when he is hungry but he makes provision for food before only."26

Thus an arhant has to be conscious and alert throughout his life to keep away from Dukkha.

It has been accepted that when one transgresses Dukkha he enters into the state of arhantship or निब्बाणं. Therefore now the question is: does Dukkha penetrate into this state of spiritual bliss? King Milinda had a question pertaining to this point.

He questioned, "Is Nibbāṇa a complete happiness or mixed with Dukkha?" [27] The answer is, "Nibbāṇa is complete happiness (एकन्तसुखं) and not mixed." King Milind said, "I do not believe it for I feel that it is mixed with sorrow. The reason is that those who have achieved nibbāṇa, suffer from bodily or mental tormentations. They squeeze all the spheres of the five sense organs (पञ्चेद्रियं) and thereby close, cut all the forms of pleasure. Thus they torment their body and mind; owing to this they suffer from bodily (कायिकदुक्खवेदनं) and mental pain (चेतसिकदुक्खवेदनं). For this reason I say that Nibbāṇa is mixed with Dukkha."

Rev. Nagasena argued, "No, you are mistaken, sire; you talk about the earlier phase of निब्बाणं but when one obtain nibbāṇa, experiencesns it then it is only complete happiness and not mixed with Dukkha." He gives a simile. A king who before obtaining a kingdom has to fight with enemies, travel in the storm or in jungle where mosquitos bite, animals harass; but once he becomes the ruler he enjoys only happiness of Kingship and there is no suffering, no sorrow at this state. Similarly nibbāṇa is a state of complete happiness not mixed with Dukkha."

He further explained [28] "Nibbana is complete happiness and not mixed with Dukkha; Dukkha is one thing and nibbana is another thing" (अञ्ञं दुख्खं, अञ्ञं निब्बाणं) For this he gives the example of a teacher who has to undergo many troublesome duties. This part of life is earlier (पुब्बभागो) and sorrowful. But when he becomes a teacher he enjoys the happiness of teaching. It is only सुखं with no mingling of दुक्खं. So निब्बाणं is only एकन्तसुखं।"

Thus the points raised in the Milinda Pañha are pertinent, intelligent and human. The answers given to these questions are similarly based on a subtle level of philosophy. On the contrary the gathas of the monks and nuns are based on a gross level of philosophy. Milind pañha talks about Dukkha, by taking into account Pañña, Vedanā, Kāyikadukkha Vedanā, Cetasikadukkha Vedanā, etc., but fails to show us the direct path that would lead one to get rid of Dukkha. One may feel that King Milinda is giving a let-out to the doubts of a discerning common man. Perhaps the questions of the King may not reach to the roots of Dukkha but they certainly help us to know the boundaries of Dukkha. I think his is a plus point of the book; for it eventually helps us to understand the Dukkha.

References

1. W. Winternitz, *History of Indian literature*, Vol,II, Calcutta, 1933, p.111.
2. *Ibid.*
3. N.K.Bhagwat, *Theragatha*, Bombay, Unpublished, 1939, Bombay p.54.
4. *Ibid.*,p.56.
5. *Ibid.*,p.73.
6. *Ibid.*,p.112.
7. *Ibid.*,p. 122.
8. *Ibid.*,p. 90
9. *Ibid.*,p. 83
   *अब्बुहि वत मे सल्लं दुद्दसं हदयनिस्सितं।
10. एकमन्त उपाविसिं। अज्वलरा फिकखूणी, *Ibid*, p.8, verse 70.

11. रत्तिया पुरिगे यामे पुब्बजातिमनुसरं, रत्तिमा मज्जिमे यामे दिब्बचकखु विसोधयुं। वत्तिमा पच्छिमे यामे तमोकखन्धं पदालयुँ तिसंमत्ता थेशीकिकसुणियो, *Ibid.*,p.13.
12. Ibid.,p.verse
13. अरियट्ठङ्गिक मग्गो निरोधो फुसितो मया। Ibid.P.13
14. *Ibid.*,p.5
15. *Ibid.*,p.15
16. *Ibid.*,p.16
17. *Ibid.*,p.17
18. *Ibid.*,p.21
19. *Ibid.*,p.27
20. *Ibid.*,p.9
21. *Ibid.*,P.37
22. *Ibid.*,p.42
23. *Ibid.*,p.44
24. *Ibid.*,p.44
25. *Ibid.*, p.89
26. *Ibid.*, p.90
27. *Ibid.*, p.287
28. *Ibid.*, 288

Vedanta and Buddhism

4

C.L.Prabhakar

"Buddham Saranam Gacchami"

'Duhkhamariyasacam' suffering is the sublime truth in Buddhism. This is real in this mundane world for all beings (pranis). Suffering has no distinction among people. In respect of all people irrespective of caste, colour, creed and status, duhkha is a common experience. It is said : 'Janma duhkham, jara yed duhkham, duhkham eva catasmat jagrata jagratta meaning birth is sorrow, old age is sorrow and hence what is sorrow, is sorrow only and it is cautioned "be careful, be careful". The real remedy lies in the expression 'Jagrata, jagrata'. The same jagrata in other words is 'Buddhatva' and that buddhatva leads to 'bodhisattvatta" in a sense stamina and resistance is developed within, owing to the knowledge of sorrow, a truth which is difficult to deny. Religions, rather various faiths arise owing to the truthful factors sorrow and fear which is a tag for all things and commodities in this world. At times sukha also is sorrow. It is enclosed as one among the twelve duhkhas in srutis. We need "awakened souls" like Sankara, Buddha and such eminent persons who elevated themselves and at the same time endeavoured through instruction (upadesa) to help others to lift themselves up. We need the gospel of Buddha, the rules for discipline, mantras to chant, behaviourial conduct and doctrines to follow at all times. More so today: all this fall under the net Vedanta. Veda is knowledge and anta is goal. The goal of knowledge is to practise the means and measures to redeem oneself from the clutches of sorrow. It is said : "Vicāranīyā Vedānta and vaṅdanīya guravaḥ. So to relieve oneself from sorrow, the outlet is : discussion and service (pariprasnena sevaya). Hence, it is advised the vedantic precepts and concepts have to be put for discussion and thinking. It is hoped the truth becomes revealed owing to that activity (vāde vāde jāyate tattva bodhaḥ).

Buddhism is a world religion like Hinduism or Christianity which contains oceanic literature both religious and philosophicl. Slowly the man should be brought into the network of Vedanta and be urged to put forth efforts individually or in groups (sangham) for spiritual happiness and peace. He has to be advised to eliminate the animal in him. The various pitakas in Pali which Buddhism follows, cover suggestions to avert evil, practise good works and enter into the portals of peace, bliss, happiness, etc; finally attain nirvana whereafter there is no return (napunarāvttih). The underlying solution is dharma *pari palana* and seeking absolute refuge in it (dhammamsaranam gacchāmi).If dharma is understood, responsibilities are understood and realised. So dharma is a warranted factor. Dharma is duty by nature and responsibility to discharge. Bhagavan Buddha preached in favour of dharma viz., manushya dharma. That dharma refers to self and group, also to follow animals. Their welfare adds to human prosperity. If self alone is looked at, that would be condemned as a self-centred activity and ego-bound deeds. Aham (ego) should be suppressed. So one need to be cautious and conscious in the matter of dharma. The Buddha's teaching refers to dharma.

Man is known for desires (kama). If desires are kept under control and if they are to refer to dharma kama 'they promote happiness which is the goal of human existence. The desires when justified are called' satya kamāh. Bhagavan Buddha basically said "have discretion on desires". Those which are detrimental, violent, etc., be ruthless to kill and thus obviate them totally. Mind is the base for desire so he advises mind-control. The instructions by the Buddha are on an instalment basis and at a level of commentator's understanding. Man is a unit for religion not his antecedents. The moment he saw the truths of life upon the earth, he started to communicate. None but

(God), a noble person (all intelligent) would come out with ethical generality. He, as an Enlightened soul, came out with the desire for universal good. Bhagavan Buddha had five disciplies with whom he began instructions at Saranath near Kasi and today it is a great pathway for liberation for all human good, a well trodden way since centuries together.People realised that there is no end to suffering and it should be stopped howsoever. For that Vedanta is the only outlet. Vedanta preaches 'thyāga; priti for general good. Our Indian method is to hit upon truths, means and measures through dialogues and knowledge and experience given out by gurus. Guru and sisya, rather preceptor and sadhaka, are the medium for the outgrowth of knowledge. The acarya is capable to clear the doubts in the mind of pricchaka and urge him to practise truths freed from doubts. An acarya is one who in true sense practises the doctrines by himself and instructs the same with a note of his anubhava for the benefit of followers. It is said : *samsayatma vinasyati*. Doubts lurking in the mind make the individual perish. So one should clear one's doubts and be a jñāni. As is said, four kinds of people look for support, materialistic and spiritual. Ārtī, jijnasuḥ, artharthi, moksharthica viz. he who wants money (wealth), knowledge, and who wants to be relieved of sorrow and who wants nirvana, these people turn to gurus (preceptor) like Buddha or Sankara. There is always a duality which confronts seekers. Duality is a problem. Decision and knowledge in that respect is śanti. It is said, rise above dualities. It is not easy to understand the controversy; still efforts should be made. Thyagaraja, a vaggeya kara of 17th century poses a question to God to answer that he only should clear his doubt, whether he is the lord of Uma or lord of Ma(Lakshmi). The answer could be : the base is the mental set-up. Acordingly the truths get uncovered and revealed. It is the envisage of the wise like the Buddha and others to explain both and leave the mind of seekers free to decide after due judgement. The Buddha suggests: use discretion and act.

Religion is a matter of choice; philosophy is a matter of understanding of it such that the evil sins, fears and the sorrows are relieved, happiness is ensured here. The Buddha came out with his Vedanta view viz., to stop sorrow gradually. He said at one place: "let all sins of all my devotees come to me and let I alone suffer. Let people be happy." This kind of preaching is a matter of hope to seekers. It is like telling *"loke yāni pāpāni Vishu santiani mām prapnuvantu.*" A soul who has such an attitude and sacrificial mind deserves to be a leader. The Buddha is a successful religious leader who influenced people worldwide. People have got to be taught the ways of living and the means for personality development. Instruction in the 'art of living' too should be given. This is a mission of Buddhism on a large scale. It is said the essence of Buddhism is contained in three principles known as sila (character), samādhi (meditation) and panna (the means to remove ignorance).

In modern times the doctrines of the Buddha are valid and relevant.People are oppressed by anixiety, confusion, stress and mental tensions. The teachings of the Buddha which are quite vedantic in spirit urge the seekers to acquire stability of mind and strength of soul. Certain rigidities in religious practices of other religions are relaxed in this religion. Absence of mental balance in the disciplines of people cause restlessness. No religion is without philosophy. Those religions which have no philosophy of longstanding value perished. Not even their names are known (nāmāpina sruyate). Buddhism has many thoughts akin to other world religions. The formulas are in the popular language of the contemporary times viz in pali. The awakened soul, rather the enlightened Buddha, in his previous aśrama was a prince. He came to Sangha to preach dharma. He developed disgust at the ways seen in the world, youth is not constant, old age cripples. Death threatens, sorrow is seen right from the cradle to the grave. Still with temporary happiness, people forget fear and threatening evil & misery. But Buddhà cautions *tātalika vairagya* is no good. Know the superior and care for absence of rebirth in spite of wordly things. Birthlessness, peace now and happiness at all times are the aims of Vedanta of any beneficial religion.Religion does not bother whether the prophet/preacher/ācārya is looked upon as a God or an ordinary being with realized mind and spirit. If the doctrines are followed, happiness is certain. The true Vedanta lies in negation and progress to arrive at nirvana. Sankara's nirvana, shatka is applicable to the online thinking of the Buddha and the fact is to be realised that the individual is freed from all strings of attachment. Live a normal life although life is a variety of experiences. No one is always praised or criticized, still the dharma in a beneficial way must be pursued and instructed to the needy.

Like in Vedanta in Buddhism also the pursuit of knowledge, awareness of relevant knowledge formed a solution for the removal of suffering. Absence of knowledge is a matter of suffering. Lack of control of mind and the senses is another lacuna. In Buddhism there are bodhisatvas who show awareness of knowledge and impart skills to the benefit of mankind. There are mantras like in the Veda and Hinduism which are effective. Mantras are texts or expression which are generative of powers. They generate vibrations which take the shape and styles in Humans by providing mental rest and happiness free from further agony. Actually duhkha is one side of the coin and relief of the same is the reverse side of the coin. We look for Vedanta for relief from sorrows. Physical duhkha is different from mental and spiritual discomfort. Physical can be continuous. It can be expiated. What is Vedanta, it is truth. The term is translated into English rightly thus as Philosophy (love for wisdom). In order to explore the truths and rewards, religion is a sadhana and hence like the dual terms we say religion and philosophy go hand in hand. Every religion is a mode and its philosophy is the science and realisation.

The aim of the Vedanta marga is to print out all about the 'Great' (Brahma) and attempt to be that or at least to prepare to become 'that'. What good that is a matter of investigation and it is unending. Still definitions and attempts for understanding need to be made. Let us note the statements like : *Prajnanam Brahma* 'meaning supreme awareness and absolute knowledge is Brahma. The reward for such pursuit is indicated thus: *'yobrahma vidah telokān taranti sayujyan vindanti.'* Lalitha sahasranama text says describing Gooddess to be : *'sarva Vedanta samvedya'*, meaning Goddess or para Brahma or the goal of pursuit in all religions is a form of truth, bliss and which is another term for nirvāṇa.

Our scriptures say that sakti is the chief principle for the activity in the universe. In order to know the sakti who manifests as 'iccha, jnana and kriyasakti, the expediency of the Vedanta marga becomes imminent. The famous Lalita sahasranama, a portion from the uttarakhanda of Brahmandapurana of Hindu literature, describes sakti to be comprehensible through the device of all kinds of Vedanta including the Buddha pantha (sarvavedanta samvedya). That shakti is bliss personified, thus as *nitya ananda svarupini*. She is filled in mind (chin maya) and bearing the entity of the form of absolute bliss.

What is the method through which the goal of Vedanta is realized? For that the Taittariya Upanishad answers thus : "Tapasa brahma vijijvnasaswa tapobrahmete" meaning all in all tapas is a measure to know Brahman, to know the truth and to know the status of bliss. Self is an esteemed source in an individual, Basically it is pure and elevated. One can attempt to see true self in one's own self through the methods of upasana and other meditational practices. Kalidasa, describing Lord Shiva, said Lord Shiva is always engrossed in perceiving the forms in his own self. Since that appears to be a long drawn process, the same is said that "Atmani Atmanam avaloka yantam Sadasivam". Siva is depicted also in meditational postures. That he would be dwelling with sakti in union while the vice versa also has been a truth, paramatma would not tolerate śakti going away from him and buddhatva margasba are complimentary terms meaning to know and be aware. For these pursuits a sense of detachment and attachent is needed and that grouped preferential aspect viz Vedanta. Acārya Sankara said:vedo nityam adhiyatam. Also he said : Vetaraniya Vedanta. 'The Vedantic doctrines are to be discussed while the vedic dictums are just to be followed. Here the veda refers to useful approrisms. One is a problem (samhita) and the other is individualized, individual is a unit in Vedantic pursuits. The purview of Vedanta is to be aware of the knowledge on body, mind, and spirit and the environment and if one is placed in it then it is said: Buddham saranam gacchami. 'Dharmam Saranam Gacchami, Sangham saranam gacchami. śaranu (surrender) is a key-note of happiness. Before the feet of jñāni, the higher person, one has to submit oneself by giving up one's ego, then happiness flows. This is the nucleus of Vedanta in Buddhism too. Nothing is ours. Śaraṇāgati is a paddhati, preached in all religions including Buddhism. It is no harm to submit to a capable jñāni who is called Buddha, the awakened soul. In creation, irrespective of caste, colour and creed, people are clamouring with confusion, sorrow, dismay, misery, disappointment, fear, hopelessness, etc., and hence they are restless and remain in want of relief from these. That is not the state of peace and happiness. A remedy for such is a need. This is a pathway for the saranāgati formula. In the Bhagavadgita, Arjuna adopts this mode when he says: sisyaste aham śādhi mām prapannam. Sisyatva and prapannatva are the qualification for progress in the Vedantic way. These are envisaged very much in the teachings of the Buddha. Emphasis is laid on mind and meditation and there is no better approach to visualize the truth than this pursuit. Moreover that formula helps to get over the physical attractions and discomforts. A yogi when he gets into samadhi lives the unawareness of suffering, a fact attested to by the Buddhistic Vedanta. The formula of negation is a sūdhana for progress. A mantra is given. Also it is like giving a stick to the elephant to carry so that its attention is fixed and it moves on a road, not taking deviating turns, more so with baby elephants. This moral is from a Buddhist story describing elephants' story and the measurs to control them.

There are certain sūtras which are so very powerful that they are able to remove all kinds of Duhkha (sarva duhkha prasamano mantrah) and that would help to get the fulfilment of nirvana. The senses in the body are like horses (indriyasvas) and they need be under control for dhajanasiddhi. The prajna paramita hridaya sutra has a mulamanta viz., 'gate gate paragate para sangata bodhisvaha' is a powerful mantra which will enable the upasakas to pass completely beyond error and go to the fulfilment of nirvana. All the Buddhas who abided by respective mantras have fully awakened into unsurpassed, complete, perfect enlightenment and acquired perfection and wisdom.

Sangham Saranam Gacchati.

Select References:

1. Pali Literature : Ancient Indian Literature an Anthology, Vol.1, Vedic Sanskrit and Pali. A Sahitya Academy Publication, New Delhi 2003, pp. 379-616 (This deals with pitakas and other relevant Buddhist literature comprensively) Anul Chandra Benerjee, etc.
2. "Thus Spake : The Buddha" by Swami Sudhasatvananda, Sri Ramakrishna Muth, Madras.
3. An Evaluation of the Vedantic Critique of Buddhism by Gregory J Darling.
4. Early Buddhism and the Bhagawadgita by Kashinath Upadhyay.
5. Nirvana Shatka by Sankara where negation is proposed and self to be blissfilled being emphasized. (Sadanandarupassivoharm).
6. Buddhist and Vedic studies by Wijesekhara, Ceylon.

7. The doctrine of the Upanishads and Early Buddhism by Hermann Oldenberg.
8. The Vedantic Buddhism of the Buddha by J.G. Jennings.
9. A survey of Buddhism by Sangharakshita.
10. Elaborations on Emptiness by Donald S.Lopez jr.
11. The doctrine of Awakening by Julius Evola.
12. The Ethics of Sankara by K.N. Neelakanthan, Elayath, Calicut University, Calicut, Kerala.
13. In Buddhism too we have "Prajna paramita sutra where the thoughts concur with those of Sankara.

Treatment of Suffering in Gautama's Nyāyasūtra

5

M.K. Gangopadhyay

Besides the Buddhist, at least two orhodox systems of Indian philosophy have recognised in a similar manner the basic facts about suffering or *duḥkha*—that it is a reality, that it is the inevitable fate of livings being and that the final aim should be to annihilate it for good. These two systems are the Sāṃkhya of Kapila and the Nyāya of Gautama. The very starting point of the Sāṃkhya is that man is constantly being tormented by various forms of *duḥkha* and the justification for Sāṃkhyaśāstra lies in the fact that it offers the means for absolutely destroying them. As I propose to present in this paper the Nyāya view on suffering I shall not dilate upon the Sāṃkha view, though I cannot resist the tempation of quoting the brief but apt comment of Vācaspati Miśra as he begins the explanation of the first verse of Īśvarakṛṣṇa's *Sāṃkhyakārikā* evaṃ hi śāstraviṣayo na jijñāsyeta yadi duḥkhaṃ nāma jagati na syāt, sad vā na jihāsitam, jihāsitaṃ vā aśakyasamucchedam.

In a sense *duḥkha* may be said to be the starting point of Nyāya also. The aim of any system of philosophy or *darśana* is to provide the means for attaining liberation *(apavarga)*, and right knowledge *(tattvajñāna)* is generally regarded as the means. Accordingly, in the first *sūtra* (NS 1.1.1) Gautama also says generally that the right knowledge of the sixteen categories (as enlisted by him) leads one to liberation. But how does it ultimately lead to liberation and what exactly happens in the state of liberation ? Gautama gives the answer immediately in the second *sūtra* (1.1.2) indicating the casual sequence: right knowledge leads to the removal of false knowledge *(mithyājñāna)*; false knowledge being the cause of evil *(doṣa),* its removal leads to the removal of evil, evil being the cause of activity *(pravṛtti)*, its removal leads to the removal of activity; activity being the cause of birth *(janma)*, its removal leads to the removal of birth; and birth being the cause of suffering *(duḥkha)*, its removal leads to the removal of suffering. The argument is based on the principle that the removal of the cause results in the removal of the effect. But the statement also shows that ultimately liberation is synonymous with the removal of suffering and in the words of Uddyotakara it represents *para-niḥśreyasa* or the ultimate good *par excellence*.

It may be asked, why this emphasis on the removal of suffering? Pleasure *(sukha)* is also a fact; why should not one strive to acquire pleasure also while striving to attain absolute freedon from suffering? Vātsyāyana gives the answer with an example : Just as poisoned food, though mixed with honey, is not to be sought after, so is pleasure inseparably mixed up with suffering *(duḥkhānuṣakta)*. As we shall also see later, the idea is that there is no pleasure as such ever unmixed with suffering. Clarifying the point Uddyotakara remarks: *vivekahānam aśakyṃ kartum.*

One who wants to experience pleasure has also to experience suffering and if one wants to get rid of suffering one has also to get rid of pleasure. It is not possible to acquire or to avoid the one without the other. Regarding the inseparability of suffering and pleasure he says further it may mean *avinābhāva*, invariable companionship, wherever there is pleasure there is suffering ; or *samānanimittatā*, being caused by the same causes, whatever act as causes of pleasure also acts as causes of suffering; or *samānādhāratā*, being located in the same locus, whatever is a recaptacle of pleasure is also a receptacle of suffering ; or *samānopalabhyatā*, being experienced by the same agent, whoever experiences pleasure also experiences suffering. The supreme position of suffering is thus easily clear.

The same attitude is shown by Vātsyāyana under the ninth *sūtra* (1.1.9), though perhaps in a more poignant way. As we have already remarked, according to Gautama, liberation results from the right knowledge of sixteen categories (as enumerated in the first *sūtra*). As the commentators argue, of these sixteen again, the most important one from the viewpoint of liberation is the second one, namely, *prameya*. *Prameya* here is to be taken in a technical sense to mean twelve specific objects of knowledge, the list of which is given in the ninth *sūtra*. This list includes *duḥkha* but there is no mention of *sukha*. Vātsyāyana, justifying the non-inclusion of pleasure, says that, though the reality of pleasure is not denied, suffering alone has been mentioned to emphasise the fact that a person striving after liberation must look upon everything as nothing but suffering and then only would he be able to stop forever the continuous flow of births and deaths thereby removing totally all sufferings for good. I may well quote the orginal passage of Vātsyāyana : duḥkham it nedam anukūlavedanīyasya sukhasya pratīteḥ pratyākhyānam.kin tarhi ? Janamana evedaṃ sasukhsādhanasya duḥkhānuṣaṅgād duḥkhenāviprayogād vividhabādh-anāyogād duḥkham iti samādhibhāvanam upadiśyate. samāhito bhāvayati, bhāvayan nirvidyate, nirviṇṇasya vairāgyam, viraktasyāpavarga iti. Janmamaraṇprabandhocchedaḥ sarvaduḥkhaprahāṇam apavarga iti.

The idea that the removal of suffering should be the prime motive for us is also evident in Gautama's simple definition of liberation (*apavarga*), the ultimate goal of human existence Thus, in the twenty-second *sūtra* (1.1.22) he says that liberation is the absolute deliverance from suffering *(tad-atyanta-vimokso 'pavargaḥ)*. This deliverance is absolute, because it is sure and non-recurring. Ordinary removal of pain is not so. A disease, for example, *may be* or *may not* be cured by a particular medicine. Again, even if it is cured, there is no guarantee that it will never recur. But, in liberation, suffering is definitely removed by right knowledge and it is never produced again.

In the commentary, Vātsyāyana once again emphasises that this birth, this very human existence, is synonymous with suffering. He says :

"The absolute deliverance from it, i.e. from suffering- and therefore from birth — is liberation. What is the implication ? The giving up of the birth which has already taken place and the non-acceptance of any other. Such a state, when it continues for ever without an end, is known as liberation to those who know the true nature of liberation (*apavargavid*). It is a state of fearlessness (*abhaya*), without decay and death (*ajara*) ; it is what the scriptures call *brahman* and it is the attainment of the highest good."

Vātsyāyana has also elaborately refuted the view that eternal bliss is manifested in the state of liberation. It may be objected that if liberation is said to be only the removal of suffering a person would not be sufficiently induced to strive for liberation, because one is generally led to activity not for just avoiding the undesirable but rather for acquiring the desirable. Thus, if there is no happiness or pleasure to be attained in liberation, why should one try to achieve it ?

Vātsyāyana answers that there is no invariable rule that one is motivated only by the desire for obtaining the desirable ; one may as well be motivated by the desire for avoiding the undesirable. In fact, what happens in the case of a pe-son truly eager to attain liberation is that he actually realises that nothing that is desirable is ever unmixed with the undesirable and, as a result, even the desirable amounts to the undesirable. One trying to reject the undesirable (i.e.suffering) also rejects the desirable (i.e.pleasure) as well, because selective rejection (*vivekahāna*) is impossible.

Finally, let us see briefly what Gautama and Vātsyāyana say in the section on the critical examination of suffering *duḥkha-parīkṣa-prakaraṇa* in the first *āhnika* of the fourth *adhyāya* of the *Nyāyasūtra*. According to Vātsyāyana, Gautama follows a three-step methodology in the discussion of the categories. Thus, suffering is first named (*uddeśa*) in NS 1.1.9 as a *prameya* ; secondly, it is defined (*lakṣaṇa*) in N.S. 1.1.21 as being of the nature of pain (*bādhanā*); and thirdly, its nature is critically examined (*parīkṣā*) in detail in NS 4.1.54-57.

The first point Gautama makes in this section is that any kind of birth simply means being afflcted with different kinds of pain constantly, and one who realises this fact ultimately gets liberated. As Vātsyāyana explains :

"Pain again is of different kinds–mild (*hīna*), moderate (*madhyama*) and severe (*utkṛṣṭa*) pain experienced by those condemned to hell is severe ; pain experienced by the human beings is mild ; and pain experienced by the gods as well as those free from attachment is milder.

"Thus, finding that all the regions in which the living beings are born are inseperably connected with different kinds of pain, a person specifically determines that pleasure as well as the means for obtaining it, namely, the body, the sense-organs and the mind are to be looked upon as suffering only.

"Next, because of specifically determining that the body, etc., are to be looked upon as suffering only, he has the knowledge— with regard to pleasure, etc., attainable in all the different worlds (namely, the fourteen *bhuvanas* from *satyalaka* to *avīci*) — that 'these pleasures etc., do not constitute my desirable ends (*anabhirati*).

"When he repeatedly meditates upon the knowledge that 'pleasure, etc., do not constitute my desirable ends, he becomes free from the craving for the enjoyment of pleasure in respect of all the different worlds and due to a total annihilation of the cravings for the enjoyment of pleasure, he is delivered from all kinds of suffering. This is similar to the case of one who ascertains some quantity of milk to be nothing but poison due to its contamination by poison, does not take it up for drinking and because of not taking it up, does not have to suffer death".

The other point made by Gautama is that the ordinary people cannot differentiate between suffering and pleasure and wrongly consider the various forms of suffering as pleasure. They are to be freed form this misconception and it is the duty of the Śāśtrakara to advise them properly. Again we may quote Vātsyāyana :

"It has been prescribed that pleasure and body, etc., are to be meditated upon as suffering only.

"An ordinary person bent upon the enjoyment of pleasure alone thinks wrongly that pleasure is the highest goal of human life, that there is no ultimate good except pleasure, and when he attains pleasure, he considers that the mission of his life is fulfilled, that he has accomplished what a human being ought to achieve in the human life.

"Due to false deliberation, he gets firmly attached to pleasure and the means for obtaining it, namely, the objects of enjoyment; being so attached, he strives for attaining pleasure and ultimately, there are produced various kinds of suffering due to birth, old age, diseases, death, obtaining what is not desired, separation from what is desired and not receiving what is sought after. And he wrongly considers all these kinds of suffering to be pleasure only. Suffering is indeed an inseperable part of pleasure, for it is impossible to obtain pleasure without being afflicted by suffering. Thus, due to such invariable dependence (of pleasure on suffering), an ordinary person (wrongly ascertains suffering as pleasure)..... and having his critical faculty impaired by such a false notion, he runs through the process of recurring births and deaths, and can never move out of the bondage of wordly existence.

"For this reason, as a repellent to the wrong notion identifying suffering with pleasure, it has been prescribed that pleasure and the body, etc., are to be meditated upon as suffering only."

From the above it is clear that the supreme position of suffering in the system of philosophy—with reference to bondage and freedom—is recognised by the Nyāya also. Like some of the other important ancient systems, it also lays special emphasis on the fact of suffering and endeavours in its own way to indicate the way out of it. It is also remarkable that though the two systems, the Nyāya and the Buddhist, are more in opposition than in agreement so far as the basic philosophicl issues are concerned appear to hold, at least in the case of suffering or *duḥkha*, a view that may be commonly acceptable. In fact, when one goes through some of the relevant orginal passages in the commentaries of Vātsyāyana and Uddyotakara and notices the use of some particular terms and the manner of presentation----- one may not fail to notice that both in style and content they may almost be considered as good as a Buddhist account.

It is well known that the relation between the Sāṃkhya and the Buddhist as well as the problem of dependence of one system upon another has been the subject of discussion by many a scholar. We have already noted that the very starting point of the Sāṃkhya is suffering. Thus, if we accept the more or less generally accepted view that the Sāṃkhya is the earliest system of Indian Philosophy, we may say that the view of the supremeness of suffering was first advocated by the Sāṃkhya, it was nourished, developed and brought to culmination by the Buddhist and when the Nyāya found it relevant for its philosophical stand it adopted it, may be, in its own way.

Dukkham Aryasaccam as Depicted in The Buddhist Nikaya and Agamas

6

S.K. Pathak

I

Among the academics the resurgence of Buddhist Studies had been inaugurated by Thomas William Rhys Davids by the last quarter of the nineteenth century A.D. Alike to accidental material industrial inventions by scientists, Thomas William Rhys Davids explored the huge treasure of the Buddhist Nikaya literature of Pali in Shri Lanka (then Ceylon). A story behind that exploration was wounderful. The British Magistrate had to deal with a court case of litigation in which the documents had been in the Pali language, what was then a wonder to the Britishers there. The said Magistrate succeeded to be conversant in the old Singhalese language Pali with the guidance of the Ceylonese Buddhist eminent scholar Je Unnanan thoroughly. That may be epitheted as the scriptural exploration of Orientalism in the nineteenth century A.D.

In 1875 the learned article on the ancient Ceylonese scripts used during Parakrama Vahu in the Journal of Royal Asiatic Society, London by T.W. Rhys Davids did announce what was Pali in the academic world. Immediately after that the said author focused on in the JRAS, London the Pali Tripitaka Nikaya literature from the Theravada Buddhist shrine in Srilanka.

Since then, the Nikaya literature became an important source of Budhist Studies. In does not mean the studies on the Nikayas had been abandoned prior to that venture by T.W. Rhys Davids. But, those studies were limited among the Buddhist monastic members of a *parivena* and extended as far as the devout Buddhists of Sihala, Suvannabumi, Suvannadipa and the Malaya achipelago. The contribution of Mathew Arnold's name the Light of Asia and that of Mrs Rhys Davids Gautama the Man could introduce the personality of Gautama, the Buddha, to the then western world.

The paper attempts to examine how suffering becomes a prime truth *dukkham ariyasaccam* as that is depicted in the Pali Nikaya literature and that is in the Agama Literature available in Chinese translation. For analysis of the problem the paper is distributed in four sections investigating the nature of suffering and its quantum for the suffering as a prime truth in this conventional world prevails on all sentient beings of the humans.

II

Nature of suffering

Despite the repeated expression *dukkham ariyasaccam*, suffering as a prime truth the Tripitaka literature in Pali and the Agama texts available in their Chinese versions, except the latter's occasional citations in the Sanskrit Sutra and Vinaya texts, do not define what is *dukkha*. The descriptions of the suffering, as an incontrovertible fact *saccam / satyam*, are the following; (1) Birth is suffering, (2) Decay is suffering, (3) Disease is suffering (4) Death is suffering, (5) A company with a non-cherished one is suffering (6) Separation from a cherished one is suffering and , (7) Wish being unfulfilled becomes suffering 8. In brief, five aggregates are suffering.

The Dhammacakka pavattana sutta reads :
idam kho pana bhikkhave dukkham ariyasaccam, jati pi dukkha, jara pi dukkha, vyadhi pi dukkha, maranam pi dukkham, appiyehi samayogo dukkho, piyehi vippayogo dukkho, yampiccham na labhati tampi dukkham, sankkhittena pancupadanakkhandha dukkha.

The above is described in the first discourse of Gautama, the Buddha at the Deer Park of Saranatha, nearby Varanasi.

The eightfold enunciation may be reviewed as common for being an inescapable (better, uncontradictable) fact in respect to an animate being. So suffering is that which is *saccam / satyam*. In other words, Gautama the Buddha might have cited the instance of suffering, which is common to all in elucidation of the thesis of *hetu-phala* the cause and effect, in either generating or degenerating, by the successive descending order or in the reverse ascending order *anuloma-patiloma*.

The said *sutta* adds that suffering has also cause(s) and thus the cause of the suffering *dukkha-samudaya-ariyasaccam* is also a prime truth. He enunciates the craving *tanha* to follow again and again and that produces rebirth accompanied by clinging(s) or passion(s) to welcome the next. He also enumerates three kinds of craving; 1. For the senual pleasure *kamatanha*, for the existence *bhovatanha* and for the non-existence *vibhavatanha*.

Again, a cause as and when is, that it has cessation being an incontrovertible fact in the phenomenal world which appears to be of the essence and is permanent. The text teads :

idam kho pana bhikkhave dukkham ariyasaccam, yayam tanha ponobbhavika nandiraga-sahagata tatra tatrabhinandini; seyyathidam kama tanha, bhava tanha, vibhava tanha
idam kho pana bhikkhave dukkha-nirodham ariyasaccam, yo tassayeva tanhaya asesa viraga-nirodha cago patinisaggo multi analayo.

The same is read in the Dighanikaya of the Mahaparinibbana Sutta when the Buddha delivered his teachings among the inhabitants of Koti village assembled by the bhikkhusangha.

Etymologically, *dukkha / dukkha* suggests a state of discomfortable strenuous stress which becomes painful to endure by a sentient being, as opposite to *su* (good) *kha* (sate). Again *dukha* is also observed for *dukkha* in Pali in absence of *sukha*. Here, *kha* refers to *stha* in Sanskrit derived from the verbroot *stha* like *sva-stha* one's own state of being.

What is one's own state of being in respect of a sentient one ? An epistemologist may question. Gautama left the answer *multi analayo* above. He also referred to the state : "It is the complete separation from and destruction of the very craving, its forsaking renunciation, the liberation therefrom and non-attachment thereto" (Narada 1971:90). Another interpretation goes *kha* as emptiness referring to the conventional truth phenomena craving for a phenomenon becomes suffering i.e., *dukkhata*.

Gautama, the Buddha advised the king of Koshala by defining *sukham* happiness in another manner

iayam veram pasavati dukkham seti parajito /
upasanto sukham seti hitva jaya-parajayam //

(Dhammapada, Sukhavagga, verse 3)

Conquest begets enmity, the conquered live in misery; the peaceful one (who extinguishes the fire of moral defilement) lives in happiness after renouncing conquest and defeat.

The commentary here refers to a historical account of a feud between Ajatashatru, the son of King Bimbisara, and queen Videhi, the sister of the king of Koshala. That amounted to the interstruggle between the rulers of Magadha and Koshala. It may suggest that suffering is neither uniform in respect of all nor its quantum becomes equal to all. Moreover suffering is both subjective and objective as explained above.

From the above citations, it is evident that the suffering and the happiness in respect of an individual or those of a group or society are relatively conditioned. The inevitable relative factor in respect of a living being was examined by Gautama the Buddha thoroughly in his discourses repeatedly. The Nikaya texts and the Agamas refer to those teachings. The Mahayana Sutras also focus on the problem of *duhkha skandha*. The *Arthavinishcaya-Sutra*, which is regarded as one of the important treatises of the Abhidharmilka among the Sarvastivadins, elucidates that suffering is sensible alike happiness which is experienced. The text reads: *Vedana katamah/sad vedanakayah / caksusamsparshaja-vedana, sukha, duhkha a-duhkha-sukha ca / evam shotra-ghrana jihva-kaya-manah-samsparshaja vedana sukha, duhkha, a-duhkha-sukha*. (edn. Samtani 10:6).

Viryashri-datta explains the above *duhkham satyam which* refers to the threefold nature of the suffering such as, 1. Birth is suffering amounts to samkara-duhkhata, decay is suffering, because of viparinama dukhata and lastly disease in respect of an animate being is suffering on account of *duhkhaduhkhata*. (edn. Samtani 160-161).

Vasubandhu in his *Abhidharmakosha karika* and his commentary *Abhidharmakosha bhasya* (ed. P. Pradhan, Patna, 1967) elucidated the above three kinds of *duhkhata* i.e., the nature of the suffering on account of being afflicted conditionality of a phenomenon.

duhkha-s-triduhkhata-yogad-yathayogam-ashesatah /
manapa amanapashca tadanye caiva sastravah //

Abhidharmakosha VI. 3

In his self-commentary, the above threefold suffering are : *duhkha-duhkhata* suffering caused by the suffering owing to the inclination to the conditioning activites *samskara*. The conditioning activities have psychosomatic relevance in each case. Those are thereby moral, immoral, good and evil, ethical and non-ethical. Thereby they become suffering caused by the suffering at the instant of being craved and they are liable to be decayed owing to the inclination to be born, to make something, anew.

The other two appear either pleasant manapa or unpleasant *amanapa* despite being suffering by the *viparinama* resultant of causing to come into existence. That reminds the introductory remarks of Maudgalayana to Shariputra: That which originates is liable to decay by the principle of causation; thus said the Great Samana.

ye dhamma hetuppabhava hetum tesam tathagata aha /
tesam ca yo nirodho evamvadi mahassamana //

(Vinayapitaka : Mahavagga 1.10)

The Buddhist Psychology like the Abhiddhamma texts *Dhammasangani* lays importance on the mind and its multiple status, inspite of its momentwise changeableness. They accumulate innumerable psychic impressions. In each fraction of a second through the psycho-somatic contact a sentient being feels the phenomena and that accumulates by the most sensitive activities performed by the mind. The mind is termed therefore *cittam* for such tendency of accumulation *ciyate iti cittam*. The Nikayas and the Agamas, despite their diverse manner in their presentation, deal with the feelings of happiness, suffering or indifference *a dukhasukha*.

With an optimistic approach the Buddha defines *sukham* happiness in relative context for the persons concerned. Such as, the exclamation came out from Goutama the Buddha while he had been invited by a house-holder gahapati during his stay at Jetavana. A bride of the who had gone to the house hones. Seeing the young bride so engaged in reception of the Buddha and his companions, her bridegroom became annoyed and displeased. On that occasion, the Buddha's utterance came out :

natthi rega-samo aggi natthi dosa-samo kali /
natthi khanda-sama dukkha natthi santiparam sukkham //

(Dhammapada Sukhavagga, verse no. 4)

There is no fire like passion, there is no evil like hatred, there is no suffering like the aggregates (of a being) *khandha/skandha;* there is no happlness that surpasses the peace. It may be noted that the Sinhalese (SriLankan) edn., and the Siamese recensions read *Khanda-disa* for *khanda-sama* above.

Also, the Dhammapada of the Khuddaka Nikaya mentions an occasion in respect to Prasenajit Koshala when Gautama the Buddha uttered, 'health (with no disease) is the greatest gift, contentment is the greatest wealth, a trusted friend is the best relative, Nibbana is the greatest bliss'.

aragya-parama labha sanfutthi-paramam dhanam /
vissasa-parama nati nibbanam paramam sukham

(Dhammapada, Sukhavagga, verse no. 6)

III

Here the Agama *o.han pu* literature of the Sarvastivadins may be taken into account in comparison to the Pitaka literature of the Theravadins for examining the concept of *dukkha* through the ages.

Historically speaking, the Pitaka literature in Pali generally refers to the concept(s) developed in the Majjhima desa traditions as those were followed in the then Bharatavarsa and in the South and the South East Asian countries since the 3rd century B.C.

Whereas, the Agama literature, which is preserved now in Chinese version only belonged to the Sarvastivadins and the Mulasarvastivadins or broadly naming the Sautrantika and the Vaibhasikas descended from the early division the Mahasanghika and the Sthavira. They flourished in the north west Bharatavarsa extending from the then Mathura (Shurasena) to Uddiyana, Gandhara, further west like Eastern Persia (Parthia), and northwest Greco-Bactrian Sogdiana and, later on, up to Central Asia and China since the Pre-Christian days. That amounted to variations in conceptual growth in the Buddhist thought. The present paper examines this with reference to *duhkha.*

An shih kao of Parthia or Arsak translated the *Dharmacakra pravartana sutra* from its Sanskrit recension in Chinese *Chwan fa lun ching* Tai Shou during his stay in China 148-170 A.D. when the Eastern Han Dynasty was ruling there. Moreover, he prepared the Chinese version of *Dashottara dharma Sutra Chang o han shi pao fa aching* for enumerating *duhkka* as a conditioned psychic reflex out of contact, opposite to that of *sukha.*

Later on, Buddhayashas translated the *Dirghagama* in Chinese *Fo show ch'an o han ching* in collaboration with Chu Fo nien by 412-13 during the latter Tshin Dynasty A.D. 384-417.

In these texts *duhkha* is regarded as the necessary attribute of being existent in respect of a sentient being. And that is accumulated after being caused by samskara impressions resulting from action. The above interpretation refers to the characterization of duhkha as in the *Dharmacakrapravartan sutra* in connection with fourfold *aryosatya* namely duhka duhkhanirodha and nirodha marga.

Again the *Mahaparanirvana Sutra* of the Sarvastivadin *Fo pan ni yuan ching* translated by Po Fa tsui, a Chinese shramana of Honei, who appeared in Western Tshin Dynasty 265-316 A.D. Again the said text rendered into Chinese by Buddhayasa in *Fo show ch'ien o han ching* Dirghagama sutra along with other sutras. In between the above two translations, a Chinese version *Fo show fang tang ni yuan ching* was done in the Eastern Tshin Dynasty period. That Chinese version appears to be different from Fa hien's translation *ta pan nil phan ching*. Again the Chinese Shramana Fa hien rendered a text in collaboration with Buddhabhadra of India who belonged to the Mahayana tradition. From the above information, we have adequate materials to examine the conceptual change of duhkha both in the Hinayana and in the Mahayana. *Duhkha-duhkhata* is therefore accepted in the Agamas also.

The Sarvastivadin Agama texts like the Madhyamagama *chung o han ching* raised a poignant question : what is duhkha ? And, *duhkha-skandra* ? In response to them the sutra referred to the dialogue between a Brahmin (Ashvajit ?) and the Buddha Bhagavan to propound that pain *duhkha* was caused by the threefold cravings *trsna* to long for. The latter functions in the mind under *asrava* the inclination that discharges. That might be painful and troublesome *klesha* on account of the passions inclined in the mind. Therefore, *duhkha-dukhata* is experienced as suffering of the suffering until the cause of suffering is eradicated.

A Mahayanist endeavours to cleanse that discharge by meritorious deeds instead of dong evil deeds. As a result the performer enters into the Pure Land, according to the Buddha's law of cause and effect in successive order for phenomenal existence.

A common factor may be traced in both cases. That is the deed *karma*, which is performed individually or that in a group. Several sutras of the Madhyama-agama *chung o han ching* lay emphasis on the manner of cleansing by the observance of shila as the Mahasudarshana sutra of the said Agama elaborates on the merit by observing precepts. Against those merits, Tshang yi o han ching Ekottaragama enumerates ten nonmeritorious deeds leading to the suffering duhkha.

Vissuddhimagga ascribed to Buddhaghosa (5th cent. A.D.) states that, as a ripe fruit is liable to fall down from its branch, an animate being who is born suffers death. That amounts to be the primary nature of being to be aware of what is suffering.

phalanamiva pakkanam pato patam to bhayam /
evam jatanam maccanam niccam maranato bhayam // p. 123.

Gautama the Buddha therefore challenged such obligatory nature of suffering from decay or death as an exerpt from the Pali Nikaya *udanan* under the root of Bodhi tree may be cited.

Anekajati samsara sandhavissam anibbisam /
gahakarakam gavesanto dukkha jati punappunam /
gahakaraka ditthosi puna geham na kahasi /
sabba te phasuka bhagga gahakutam visamkhitam
visankhara-gatam cittam tanhanam khayamajjhaga //

Many livings have been circumbulatingin search of the maker of the abode (a living being) and the sufferings are (experienced) again and again O, Maker of the abode ! You are now detected. No further abode you would make hence. I have broken down the top of the abode with pillars to stand upon. My mind overcomes what accumulates (to be born) since my cravings become fruitless.

The quantum of suffering

The Nikaya literature lays stress on the quantum of the suffering in respect of an individualo and of a group or society while dealing with the multitude of sufferings accumulated by many cravings of the mind through aeons.

An experience of the suffering tends to sensation, vedana which may be either somatic (physiological) or psychological (mental) or both, for the contact between an object in the phenomenal world and the sense organs including the mind *manas* and other perceptive faculties like dhatu, ayatana, etc. Sensation(s) may be of three spheres happiness, sorrow, either good and evil and indifference. The contact between the phenomenal object outside and the mental faculties in various functions accumulates apperceptive *sanna* knowing by a nomenclature to differentiate the external phenomenal object from each other. So the mental empirical impressions *samkhara* in their latest stage are related to the multiple functioning of the mental faculties accumulated in each and every response to the contact. The objective world may be either animate or inanimate or both. The responsive impressions may therefore be in awareness, subliminal or in threshold in between consciousness and the unconsciousness. The social events are not secluded from such psychic operations led by direct or indirect cause(s).

The above factors amount to generate a sixfold aggregation of psychic consciousness *vinnana* related to the responses by the contact of the five sense organs and their respective bases together with the mind consciousness *mano-vinnana*, Necessarily, all these factors lead to experience the suffering of the individual or that in respect of a group of sentient beings. Those are always impersonal i.e., having no agent *atman* or doer *karta* but the continuity of functional elements *dharma santati* governed by the cause and condition *hetupratyaya*. In the Maha vedalla sutta of Majjhima Nikaya, the dialogue between Mahakottila and Sariputta may be referred in this context to understand the function of *vinnana* conducted by the cause and condition with no agent other than the aggragate of *bhandha* i.e., *puggala*.

IV

Rahula Sankrityayan's Observation

Despite the Buddha's enunciation of the measures as to how to eradicate the cause of the suffering *dukkha-samudaya-nirodha*, it is experienced always. Again, the suffering may be individual or in a group or society in the human context. Rahula Sankrityayan, an eminent Buddhist philosopher of our days, observed the propriety of the Buddha's dictum in the present day context. He located some short-comings in the enumeration of the four prime truths cattari *ariyasaccani* as discussed below.

In respect of the individual on the spiritual quest as to how to get rid of the cause of suffering it may be applicable provided those teachings are faithfully followed to become an arhat, a reverered one by attaining spiritual excellence. While its application in the socio-economic context, Gautama the Buddha's enunciation becomes handicapped. Sanskrityayan's arguments are jotted down briefly.

(i) The forerunner of the doctrine of momentariness made no experiment about the root cause of social change and that of economic condition in his time.

(ii) On the other hand, the high priests of his days like Kutadanta, Shonadanda, pivots the Brahmanic priestism though doctrinally challenged, were appreciated. Despite his occasional declaration against the social evils of his days, he tolerated the social hegemony led by the Vedic priesthood.

(iii) Except for a few instances like the case of Anathapindada's purchase of Jetavana at Shravasti of Koshala he was generally supported by the merchants, trade-guilders of Kosambi, Rajagriha, etc., on account of their profuse donation for his monastic development.

(iv) Also many affluent devotees like Vishakha, Addhakashi were sheltered by him for the same cause.

(v) The rulers like Bimbisara and Prasenjit were his followers to lead their royal control over their respective *janapada*, in spite of the occasional bloody feuds and strifes. As a result their attitude for expansion could not be resisted to aggressions on the then republican *janapadas* of the Licchavis, the Sakyas, the Koliyas later on.

The above points may require further analysis when the Buddha compares the status of the human beings to a journey of traveller(s) on a stormy dark night (*Saddharma pundarika Sutra* Mithila Institute edn. P. 21).

Dr. B. R. Ambedkar's approach

Dr. B. R. Ambedkar with his large number of followers accepted the teachings of Gautama the Buddha as a challenge against the brahaminical social discrepancy between the social outcaste and the others. His approach to the problem of the suffering in the social context was to raise the social status of mankind in respect to those who had been downtrodden and distressed. Referring to the Buddha's teachings to Simha, a soldier, Dr. B. R. Ambedkar remarks: He (The Buddha) taught that evil should be cared by the return of good. But he never preached that evil should be allowed to overpower good. (The Buddha and his Dhamma Ambedkar 509: 22824)

Deductions :

In fine, plurality is the core of Indian culture since the hoary past. That may be among either inter-institutional groups or intra-institutional factions, Hence diversities in conceptual growth with practical applications in the course of experiments in the individual-Indian life and societies are observed. In the present case the following points may be deduced with reference to the Buddha's postulate, the suffering as the prime truth, *dukkham-ariyasaccam*.

1) Until and unless the cravings or inclinations in the mind of ordinary persons are wiped out thoroughly, the above sayings of the Buddha appear true.

2) Obversely, the Buddha's dictum *dukkham aryasaccam* becomes of no-use in the case of an arhat, a Bodisattva or a Buddha who dedicates himself for the cause of others, even at the cost of his own personal life. Because, those elevated sentient beings succeed to be above the relative identity of being a grasper with an object to grasp under ignorance *avidya*, as a Buddhist holds.

3) *Dukkham ariyasaccam* appears valid as the sublime truth in respect of those who are under suffering. The proposition stands relatively to appreciate the conventional truth *sammutisacca* as long as the reality becomes phenomenal whether subjective or objective.

Bibliography

1. Textual source materials

Pali

Dighanikaya : Nagri edn. Nalanda, Bihar

Samyutta nikaya : ed. Bhikkhu Jagadist Kassap, 1956

Anguttara nikaya

Khuddaka-nikaya

Vinayapitaka

Mahavagga

Cullavagga

Dhammapada with Tibetan, ed. C.R. Lama, Sarnath Varanasi

Visuddhimagga of Buddhaghosa

Sanskrit

Arthavinishcaya-sutra } ed. N. H. Samtani

Arthavinisheaya-sutra Nibadhana } Patna, 1971

Abhidharmasamuccaya of Asanga (restored from Chinese version) P. Pradhan, Visva-Bharati, Santiniketan 1950.

Abhidharmakosha karika of Vasubandhu }

Abhidharmakosha karika bhasya of Vasubandhu . } ed. Pralhad Pradhan

Chinese

Ta pan ni yuen ching (Mahaparivana sutra, Tai sho 376)

Fo show chan o han ching (Njo. 545) Dirghagama Sutra collection.

Chung o han ching (Njo, 542)

Tsang yi o han ching (Njo, 543)

Tibetan

'Phags pa yongs su mya ngan las das pa rin po chen po theg pa chen po'imdo (Toh, Cata. 120)

'Phags pa yongs su my alas pa chen po'imdo (Toh. Cata. 124)

II In the European and the Indian Languages

Akanuma Chizen, *The Comparative Catalogue of Chinese Agamas and the Nikayas* Tokyo, 1958.

Ambedkar, B.R. *The Buddha and His Dhamma*, Buddhabhumi Publication Nagpur, 1997.

Anesaki M. *The Four Buddhist Agamas in Chinese*, Tokyo, 1908.

Bagchi, Prabodh Chandra : *India and China*, Calutta India and Central Asia, Calcutta 1955.

Banerjee A. C. *The Sarvastivada Literature*, Calcutta Uni. 19.

Bapat, P.V. (ed.) *2500 years of Buddhism*, Publication Division, Government of India, New Delhi, 1956.

Conze Edward, *Buddhism : Its Essence and Development,* Oxford, 1951.

Daw Mya Tin tr. *Dhammapada verses and stories*, Sarnath 1990 Nanjio Bunyio (compiler)

A catalogue of the Chinese Translation of the Buddhist Tripitaka (Indian edn. Classic India Publication) Delhi 1989, First edn. 1882.

Dutt. Nalinaksa, *Early Monastic Buddhism,* vol I & II 1960

— Mahayana Buddhism 1903 (Reprinted edn.)

— Some Aspects of the transition from Hinayana to Mahayana, Luzac & Company 1926.

Narada (Ven Mahathera) *The Buddha and his teachings,* Buddhist Missionary Society, Kuala-Lampr Malaysia, Fourth edn. 1988.

Nyanamohi Bhikkhu, *The Path of Purification* (Visuddhimagga in Eng. Translation) Colombo 1964.

Pande, G.C., *Studies in the Origins of Buddhism,* Allahabad 1957.

Mayeda Egaka (in Japanese Eng. Title), *A History of Formation of the Original Buddhist texts* 1964.

Hakuju Ui et al. eds. *A Complete Cataloge of the Tibetan Buddhist Canons* (Bkah-hgyur and Bstan gyur) Sendai, Japan 1934.

Hoernle, Rudolf A.F. *Manuscript Remains of Buddhist Literature found in Eastern Turkestan*, 1914.

Samdong Rinpoch, ed. *Ten Suttas from Digha Nikaya Long Discourse of the Buddha,* Burma Pitaka Association, Rangoon, Burma Reprinted Central Institute of Higher Tibetan Studies, Sarnath, 1984.

Soothill, W.E.*A Dictionary of Buddhist Chinese Terms*, London 1937.

Winternitz, M.A. *History of the Indian Literature*, Vol. II, Calcutta University, Calcutta 1934.

Waldschmidt E. *Comparative Study of the Sanskrit fragments* of *Agamas with Chinese version*. Das Mahaparinirvana Sutra, Berlin.

Research Articles

Bapat P.V. Chinese Madhyamagama and the Language of its Basic Text, Satkari Mukherjee Felicitation Volume 1969. Calcutta. The Different Strata in the Literary materials of Dighanikaya *Annals of Bhandarkar Oriental Research Institute* Vol. XXXI, 1950 Poona.

Bnrough, John.: The have I heard, *Bulletin of the School of Oriental and African Studies*, Vol. XII, 1950.

Hammalava Saddhatissa : A Survey of the Pali Literature of Thailand *Amala Prajna, Aspects of Buddhist Studies,* Professor P.V. Bapat Felicitation volume. Ed. N. H. Samtani. Delhi, 1989.

Mukherjee Bishwadib : The Relationship between the conditioned and the unconditioned according to Madhyamagama and the Upanisads, *Chung Hwa Buddhist Journal*, Taipe, Taiwan.

Gautama Becomes the Buddha : A Study in Nikaya Tradition - Chung Hwa Buddhist Journal No. 15, 2002, Taipe, Taiwan.

Prasad, Chandra Sekhar : Some Reflexions on the relation between the Agamas and the Nikayas (in) *Proceeding of the Second conference of the IABS (International Association of Buddhist Studies*, Nalanda, Jan. 1719, 1980.)

Pathak, S.K. *A note on the Dharmadhatu-garbhavivarana (Tibetan-Sanskrit translation from the Bstan 'gyur)* Indian Historical Quarterly, Calcutta 1956.

Wilemen, Charles, Survastivada and Developments in Northwest India and China, *Indian Journal of International Buddhist Studies*, 2001.

The Indian Background of Buddhism in China : Some facts and Remarks, *The Indian Buddhist Studies,* BJK Institute of Buddhist and Asian Studies, Sarnath Varanasi.

Some Problem Concerning Duhkhasatya

7

Prabal Kumar Sen

The four cardinal truths of Buddhism are *Duḥkhasatya*, *Samudayasatya*, *Nirsdhasatya*, and *Mārgasatya*. The *Satyasiddhiśāstra* of Harivarman briefly chaactrises these four truths as follows:

"दुःख सत्यमिति यत त्रैधातुकम्" (p.52) "समुदयसत्यमिति कर्मक्लेशव:" (p.55), यत् प्रशप्तिचित्तं धर्मचित्तं शून्यताचित्तमित्येषां त्रयाणां चित्तांना निरोधो निरोधंसत्यमित्युच्यते" (p.55), "मार्गसत्यमिति यत् सप्तत्रिंशत बोधिपक्षीयाधर्मा:" (p.57). The importance of these four truths has been described as follows:

"य इंद तथागतधर्मशास्त्रमध्येति स चत्वारि सत्यानि अभिसमेत्य चत्वारि श्रामण्यफलानि प्रतिलभते" (P. 57), where these four "श्रामण्यफल" viz, "स्त्रोतापत्तिफल, सकृदागामिफल, अनागामिफल" and अर्हत्फल have been associated with the progressive comprehension of these four truths. The "आर्यध्यायितमुष्टिसूत्र" as quoted in "प्रसन्नपदा" of Candrakirti on *Madhyamakaśāstra* 24/40 contains the following interesting rename:

"दुःखं परिज्ञातव्यम्। समुदयो प्रहातव्य:। निरोधः साक्षात्कर्तव्य:। मार्गो भावयितव्य:।

The *Satyasiddhiśāstra* and a number of other texts also mention that *Duhkhasatya* comprises the five *upādānaskandhas*. Thus, in chapter 36 of *Satyasiddhiśāstra,* we find the following passage:

"सत्यं नाम चत्वारि आर्यसत्यानि यदुत दुःखं दुःखसमुदयो दुःख निरोधो दुःख निरोधगामिनी प्रतिपत्। पञ्चोपादानस्कन्धा दुःखम्। कर्म क्लेशाश्च दुःखसमुदयः दुःखेक्षयो दुःख निरोधः अष्टाकिमार्गो दुःख निरोध गामिनी प्रतिपत्।" (p. 96)

The *Sarvadarśana saṅgraha* quotes the following verse from *Bodhicittavivaraṇa:*

दुःखं संसारिणो स्कन्धास्ते च पञ्च प्रकीर्त्तिताः। विज्ञानं वेदना संज्ञा संस्कारो रूपमेव च।।

A full-fledged discussion of *Duhkhasatya* thus requires an in-depth examination of the five *skandha-s*, and I hope that the learned participants of this seminar will accomplish this task in a satisfactory manner. Due to the limited time at my disposal, I have chosen to deal with the problem - does the admission of *Duḥkhasatya* imply the rejection of pleasure (*sukha*) as a real item of experience?

In the Buddhist seriptures, these four cardinal truths are also presented in the following manner.

"अस्ति दुःखम् अस्ति दुःख समुदयः, अस्ति दुःख निरोधः, अस्ति दुःख निरोधगामिनी प्रतिपत्"

Each of these four truths has four aspects ("आकार"). Thus, duhkhasatya has the four aspects "दुःखतः, अनित्यतः, अनात्मतः, शून्यतः" Thus, in verse no 1/179 of his Pramāṇa vārthica, Dharmakirti says:

कदाचिदुपलमभात् तदध्रुवं दोषनिः श्रयात्। दुःखं हेतुवशत्वाच्च न चात्मा नाप्यधिष्ठितम्।।

In his Pramāṇa vārthiravṛtti, Manorathanandī explains this verse as follows:

दुःख सत्यञ्च अनित्यतः दुःखतः शून्यतः अनात्मत श्रेति चतुराकारम् आख्यातुमाह–कदाचिदुपलम्भात् दुःखम् अध्रुवम् अनित्यम्, दोषनिःश्रयात् रागादिदोषाश्रयेणोत् पक्षेः। हेतुवशत्वाच्च।

"सर्वं परवशं दुःखम्" इति व्यायाद् दुःखं तत्। न चात्मा आश्रयम्, अनात्मतः आत्मविलक्षणत्वात्। नाप्यधिष्ठितम् अधिष्ठातुरात्मनोऽमावात्। अनेन शून्यत इत्यारव्यातम्।

In other contexts, we find the mention of त्रिविधदु:खता as दु:खदु:खता, संस्कारदु:खता and विपरिणामदु:खता. Thus, in verse no. 6/3 of his *Abhidharmakośa,* Vasubandhu says:

दु:खास्त्रिदु:खतायोगाद् यथायोगमशेषत:।

मनापा अमनापाश्च तदन्ये चैव सास्रवा:।।

तिस्रो हि दु:खता– दु:खदु:खता, विपरिणामदु:खता, संस्कारदु:खता च। ताभिर्यथायोगमशेषत: सर्वे सास्रवा: संस्कारा दु:खा:। तत्र मनाया विपरिणामदु:खतया, अमनापा दु:खदु:खतया। तेम्योऽन्ये संस्कारदु:ख तया। के पुनर्मनापा:? केऽमनापा:? के नोभमथा?

तिस्रो वेदना यथाक्रंम तद्वशेन सुखवेदनीयादयोऽपि संस्कारा मनापादि संज्ञां लभन्ते। सुखाया हि वेदनाया विपरिणामेन दु:खता। सूत्र उक्तम्– "सुखा वेदना उत्पादसुखा स्थितिसुखा विपरिणामदु:खा" इति। दु:खाया दु:ख स्वभावेनैव दु:खता। "दु:खा वेदना उत्पाद दु:खा स्थितिदु:खा स्थितिदु:खा" इति सूत्रे। अदु:खासुखा वेदनाय: संस्कारेणैव दु:खता।" प्रत्ययाभि संस्करणात् यदनित्यं तद्दु:खम्" इति।

वेदनावत् तद्वेदनीया अपि संस्कारा वेदितव्या:।

In the *Satyasiddhiśāstra* of Harivarman also, we find this three fold division of दु:ख:

यो धर्म: बाधात्मक: तद्दु:खमुच्यते। तत् त्रिविधम्–दु:खदु:खं विपरिणाम दु:खं संस्कारदु:खमिति। प्रत्युतुत्पन्ने वस्तुतो यदसिशस्त्रादि तद्दु:खदु:खम्। प्रियांणा पुनर्भार्यादीनां वियोगकाले यद्भवति दु:खंम्, इदं विपरिणामदु:खम्। शून्यतानात्मज्ञानलामिनो यच्चित्त भवति संस्कृतधर्मा: सर्वे विहेठना इति। तत् संस्कारदु:खम्। तदनुयायि चित्तं दु:खसंज्ञा। (p.434)

At another place, however, Harivarman links up the notions of अनात्मता with संस्कारदु:खता:

दु:खलक्षणं द्विविधम्–अनित्यसंज्ञोत्थितं विपरिणामदु:खलक्षणम्। अनात्मसंज्ञोत्थितं संस्कारदु:खलक्षणम्। (p. 491)

II

Several interesting questions regarding the four cardinal truths can be raised and discussed here. Consider, for example, the *order* in which the four truths have been stated. One may reasonably ask the question as to why the truth about suffering is mentioned at the beginning, and the truth about the crigination or causes of suffering is mentioned after that. A cause is followed by its effect, and not *vice versa*. Why should we not state the *samudayasatya* at the beginning, and then state *Duḥkhasatya,* so as to remain faithful to the *real* order that obtains between *Duḥkha* and *Duḥkhasamudaya*? A similar question may be raised about the order in which *Nirodhasatya* is stated before *Mārgasatya*, even though *Nirodha* is obtained only by following *Mārga*. An answer to this apparently baffling question has been provided by Vasubandhu in his *Abhidharma Kośa* and *Abhidharma Kosabhasya*. The second verse of the sixth *Kośasthāna* of *Abhidharmakośa* runs as follows:

सत्यान्युक्ताति चत्वारि दुःख समुदयस्तथा।
निरोधमार्ग इत्येषां यथाऽभिसमयं क्रमः ।। 6/2।।

Thus, for Vasubandhu, these truths are comprehended in a certain sequence, and while mentioning these truths, the order in which their comprehension (अभिसमय) takes place has been adopted. The auto commentary on this verse mentions an important point, viz, the instructions of Buddha do not follow any uniform pattern:

य्रस्य हि सत्यस्याभिसमयः पूर्वस्तस्य पूर्वनिर्देशः। इतरथा हि पूर्वं हेतु-निर्देशोऽभविष्यत्, पश्चात् फलनिर्देशः। केषाञ्चिदुत्पत्त्यनुकूला देशना, यथा स्मृत्युपस्थापनध्यानादीनाम्। केषाञ्चित् प्ररूपणानुकूला देशना, यथा सम्यक्प्रहाणानाम् ......सत्यानां त्वभिसमयानुकूला देशना।

(*Abhidharmakośa* with *Bhāṣya* and *Sphuṭārthā*, ed. by Dwarikadas Shastri, Bauddhabharati, Varanasi, Vol. III, p. 872)

In his autocommentary, Vasubandhu also draws our attention to the fact that the distinction between *Duḥkhasatya* and *Samudayasatya* that is suggested by these two expressions is only apparent, since both of them hold good of the five *upādānaskandhas*. The distinction between *Nirodhasatya* and *Mārgasatya* is, however, real or genuine:

तत्र फलभूता उपादानस्कन्धा दुःखसत्यम्। हेतुभूताः समुदयसत्यम्, समुदेत्यस्मादिति कृत्वा। अतएव तयोः फलहेतुभावान्नामतो भेदः, न द्रव्यतः। निरोधमार्गयोस्तु द्रव्यतोऽपि। (Ibid., p. 873)

(Harivarman also says - पञ्चोपादानस्कन्धा दुःखम् (*Satyasiddhiśāstra*, p. 96)

In this connection, we may ake note of a serious controversy about the number of cardinal truths and the manner in which they are comprehended. We have noted the view of Vasubandhu, who maintains that these truths are comprehended in a seqence, i.e. they are not comprehended simultaneously. Some Abhidharma teachers, however, held the view that all these four truths are comprehended in a single moment - there is no gap between their comprehensions. The *Satyasiddhiśāstra* of Harivarman has recorded this difference of opinion in the following manner:

शास्त्रमाह– केचिद् वदन्ति चतुर्णां सत्यानामनुपूर्वेणाभिसमय इति। केचिद् वदन्ति– एकक्षणेनेति। केन कारणेनोच्यते अनुपूर्वेणाभिसमयः, केन कारणेन एकक्षणेनाभिसमय इति। अनुपूर्वेणाभिसमयः। ययोक्तं सूत्रे– लोकस्य समुदयं पश्यतो नास्तिताहष्टिर्न भवति। लोकस्य निरोधं पश्यताऽस्तिताहष्टिर्न भवति इति। यः प्रजानाति--यत् समुदयलक्षणं तत् सर्वं निरोधलक्षणमिति। तस्य विरजं वीतमलं धर्मचक्षुर्भवति। आहंच–

अनुपूर्वेण मेधावी स्तोकं स्तोकं दिने दिने।
कर्मारो रजतस्येव निर्धमेन्मलमात्मनः।। इकति।।

आस्रवक्षयसूत्रमाह– जानतः पश्यतः आस्रवाणां क्षयो भवति इति। प्रतिपक्षुः प्रतिदिनं क्षीयमाणं स्वयमजानतोऽपि सदा भावितत्वात् आस्रवाणां क्षयो भवति। भगवानाह– सत्येषु उदपद्यत चक्षुः ज्ञानं विद्या प्रज्ञा इति। कामधातुकदुःखे द्वौ क्षणौ रूपारूप्यधातुकदुःखे च द्वौ। एवं समुदायादावपि सूत्रे च भगवान् कण्ठत आह– अनुपूर्वेण सत्याभिसमय इति। यथा पुरुषः श्रेणिमारूह्य उपर्यारोहति। इत्यादि सूत्राज् ज्ञायते–चतुस्सत्यानि नैककालिकानि इति।.............. योगी च चित्तं समाधाय 'इदं दुःखं' 'अयं दुःख निरोधः' 'इयं दुःखनिरोधगामिनी प्रतिपत्' इति विकल्पयेत्। यधेकस्मिन् चित्ते स्यात्, कथमेवमनुपूर्वेण समाधिविकल्पो भवेत्। अता ज्ञायते– अनुपूर्वेणाभिसमयो नैकक्षणेन।

केचिदाहुः – चतुर्णां सत्यानामभिसमयो नानुपूर्वेणेति। भवानाह– लोकस्य समुदयं पश्यतो नास्तिताहष्टिर्न भवति। लोकस्य निरोधं पश्यतो अस्तिताहष्टिर्न भवति–इति। तदा स्वमंत विनश्येत्। तथा चेत् षोडशभिः चित्तक्षणैः द्वादशभिराकारैश्च मार्गो लभ्यत इति न स्यात्। भवतोक्तं यत् समुदयलक्षणं सर्वं तन्निरोधलक्षणमिति प्रजानतो धर्म चक्षुर्भवतीति। तथा चेत् चित्तद्वयेण मार्गलाभः स्यात्– आद्यं समुदयचित्तं द्वितीयं निरोधचित्त- मिति। न त्वेतद् युक्तम्। भवानाह– अनुपूर्वेण मेधावी... निर्धमेन्मलमात्मन इति। अनेनापि न स्यात् षोडशमात्तै श्चित्तक्षणैरिति। भवतोक्तम्– आस्रवक्षय- सूत्रमाह रूपादीन जानतः आस्रवाणां क्षयो भवति। एवञ्चां प्रमाणचित्तानि स्युः, न तु षोडश चित्तमात्राणि। भवतोक्तम्– चक्षुर्ज्ञानं विद्या प्रसेति। भगवान् स्वयं ब्रवीति-चतुर्षु सत्येषु चक्षुर्विद्या ज्ञानं प्रसोदपद्येति, न ब्रवीति– अनुपूर्वेण षोडश चित्तक्षणानि भवन्ति–इति। भवतोक्तम्–भगवान कण्डनाह–अनुपूर्वेण सत्याभिसमयः श्रेण्यारोहणवत् –इति। नाधीतमिंद सूत्रमस्माभिः। सत्वेऽपि। निराकर्तव्यमेव। धर्मलक्षणाननुंगमात्।

..........................भवानाह– समाध्या विकल्पयेदिति। रूपादावपि तथा विकल्पयेत्। अतो न षोडशैव चिराक्षणाः स्युः।

योगिनो न नाना सत्यानि भवन्ति, किन्तु एकमेव सत्यं भवति, यदुत दुःख निरोधदर्शनमाद्याभिसम्बोधिनामकम्। दृश्यधर्मदिनां प्रतीत्य– समुत्पन्नत्वात् योगी उष्मगतादिधर्मापूर्वेण चरम निरोधसत्य रूपं सत्यं पश्यति। निरोध सत्य दर्शनान्मार्ग लाभ इत्याख्यायते।

(*Satyasiddhiśāstra* of Harivarman - Vol. I, Sanskrit Text), ed. N. Aiyaswami Shastri, Oriental Institute, Baroda, 1975, pp. 78-80.)

From the last paragraph of the rather long passage quoted above, we come to know the somewhat startling fact that according to some of the Abhidhārmikas, there was only *one* noble truth - the *Nirodhasatya*. Such a view is found in *Visuddhimagga* of Buddhaghosa, and Harivarman also seems to be in favour of it (see chapter 190 of *Satyasiddhiśāstra.)*

III

We may now have a brief discussion about the four aspects (*ākāra*) of *Duḥkhasatya*. These four aspects (viz. दुःखतः, अनित्यतः, अनात्मतः and शून्यतः) present, so to say, the different facets of *Daḥkha* as understood by the Buddhists, and indicate to some extent the richness and depth of the concept of *Duḥkha*. Once again, we turn to *Satyasiddhiśāstra* of Harivarman for a lucid exposition of these issues:

(i) अनित्यसंज्ञा यदनित्ये अनित्यमिति समाहितः प्रजानाति। कस्मात् सर्वनित्यम्। सर्वे हि धर्माः प्रतीत्य समुत्पन्नाः। हेतु प्रत्ययविनाशात् सर्वे अनित्यतां यान्ति।... (p.430)

अनित्यसंज्ञा श्रद्धा किं करोति। क्लेशान् विनाशयति। यथोक्तं सूत्रे– अनित्यसंज्ञा भाविता बहुलीकृता सर्वं काम रागं पर्यादाति। सर्वं रूपरागं पर्यादाति। सर्वं भवरागं पर्यादाति, सर्वमस्मिमानं पर्यादाति, सर्वमविद्यां पर्यादाति। ...... (p.432)

(ii) दुःखसंज्ञां भावयता किं हितं लभ्यते। दुःखसंज्ञायां फलान्निर्वेदो भवति। कस्मात्। न हि दुःखसंज्ञां भावयित्वा कामप्रीतिं सेवते। तत्प्रीत्यभावान्न तृष्णा भवति। .... (p. 434)

(iii) अनात्मसंज्ञया हि योगिनश्चित्तं विशुध्यति। कस्मात्। सर्वे हि क्लेशाः आत्मदृष्टिसम्भूताः। इदं वस्तु आत्मनो हितमित्यतः कामराग उत्पद्यते। अनेनात्मैवाभिमान जनकः। .... एवमात्मनैव सर्वे क्लेशाः समुद्भवन्ति। अनात्मसंज्ञया तु सर्वे क्लेशः विच्छिद्यन्ते। क्लेशानां समुच्छेदात् चित्तं विशुध्यति। (p.436)

(In this connection we may also note a beautiful verse of Mātṛceta, the famous author of *Adhyardhaśatakastotra*:

साहङ्कारे मनसि न क्षयं याति जन्मप्रबन्धो
नाहङ्कारेश्चलति हृदयादात्मदृष्टौ च सत्याम्।
अन्यच्छास्ता जगति च यतो नास्ति नैरात्म्यवादी
नान्यस्तस्मादुपशमविधेस्त्वन्मतादस्ति मार्गः।।

(Quoted in *Ratnakīrtinibandhāvali* edited by A.L. Thakur, K.P. Jaiswal Research Institute, Patna)

The following verses from the first chapter of *Pramānavārthika* by Dharmakīrti also enlighten us about the usefulness of *anātmadṛṣti*:

यः पश्यत्यात्मानं तत्रास्याहमिति शाश्वतः स्नेहः।
स्नेहात् सुखेषु तृष्यति तृष्णा दोषां स्तिरस्कुरुते।।226।।

गुणदर्शी परितृष्यन् ममेति तत्साधनान्युपाद।
तेनात्माभिनिवेशो यावत्तावत् स संसारे ।। 220।।
आत्मनि सति परसंज्ञा स्वपरविभागात् परिग्रह द्वेषौ।
अनयोः सम्प्रतिबद्धाः सर्वे दोषाः प्रजायन्ते ।। 222 ।।
संस्कारदुःखतां मत्वा कथिता दुःखभावना।
सा च नः प्रत्ययोत्पत्तिः सा नैरात्माहगाश्रयः ।। 254।।
मुक्तिस्तु शून्यताहष्टे स्तदर्था शेषभावनाः।
अनित्यात् प्राह तेनैव दुःख दुःखान्निरात्मताम् ।। 255।।

(iv) योगी तु इमे पञ्चस्कन्धाः शून्या अनात्मान इति भावयति। अतो न पुनस्तं पश्यति। यथोक्तं धर्ममुद्रासूत्रे— योगी भावयति रूपमनित्यं शून्यं वियोग लक्षणमिति। अनित्यमिति यत् रूपं स्वरूपतोऽनित्यम्। शून्यमिति यथा घटे जलेऽसति 'शून्यो घटः' इति वदन्ति। एवं पञ्चस्कन्धेषु नास्त्यात्मा— इत्यतः शून्या भवन्ति। एवं भावयिताऽपि शून्यः। .... (p. 497)

(For the expression, धर्ममुद्रा, consider the following passage from *Satyasiddhiśāstra:*

सन्ति च जिनशासनस्य तिस्रो धर्ममुद्राः —सर्वमनात्मा, सर्वे संस्कृतधर्माः क्षणिका अनित्याः, शान्तं निरोधो निर्वाणम्। इमास्तिस्रो धर्ममुद्राः सर्वैरपि वादिभिः न शक्याः खण्डयितुम्। .... (p. 21)

We may also recall the following verse quoted in *Abhidharmakośabhāṣya :*

शून्यमाध्यात्मिकं पश्य पश्य शून्यं वहिर्गतम्।
न विद्यते सोऽपि कश्चिद् यो भावयति शून्यताम्।।

Please note also that authors like Vasubandhu, Harivarman, etc., understood *śūnyatā* primarily as *pudgalaśūnyatā,* and not as *svabhāvaśūnyatā, a la* Nāgārjuna and his followers like Āryadeva and Candrakirti:)

IV

A lot of interesting issues about *Duhkhasatya* can be raised, as is evident from the issues raised in the previous section. Due to lack of space as well as time, we now choose only *one* such issue that has led to heated debates among the different sects of Buddhism. Put in a nutshell, the problem concerned is : does the admission of *Duḥkhasatya* entail the rejection of pleasure (*sukha*) as an item of experience? This issue has been discussed thread-bare by Vasubandhu in his *abhidharmakośabhāṣya* and also by Harivarman in his *Satyasiddhiśāstra,* from which certain relevant passages will be quoted and discussed by us.

Vasubandhu raises this question while discussing the problem of *Saṁskāraduḥkhata*. If all *saṃskṛtadharmas,* i.e. the entities that are produced by causes and conditions, are to be regarded as *duḥkha,* then *Duhkhanirodhagāmini pratipat or Margasatya*, being a *saṃskṛtadharma*, would turn out to be an instance of *duḥkha*. But such a consequence is certainly undesirable, because the noble aspirants of *Nirvāṇa* do not consider *Mārgasatya* to be something inimical, and we consider something to be *duḥkha* only when it is unfavourable or inimical to us. When such aspirants look upon Nirvāṇa as cessation of all that is to be regarded as *duḥkha*, they do not consider *mārga* as something that is thus to be regarded as *duḥkha*. The point to be noted is that among the entities generated by causes and conditions, only those that are defiled (*sāsrava*) are to be considered as *duḥkha*, while *Mārgasatya,* even though samskṛta, is free from defilements (*anāsrava*). This is evident from the manner in which Vasubandhu classifies the different *dharma-s* in the first *Kośasthana* of his *Abhidharmakośa*:

सास्रवानास्रवा: धर्मा: संस्कृता: मार्गवर्जिता:।
सास्रवा आस्रवास्तेषु यस्मात् समनुशेरते।।
अनास्रवं मार्गसत्यं त्रिविधं चाप्यसंस्कृतम्।
आकाशं द्वौ निराधौ च ....।।

Thus, all *saṃskrta dharma-s*, with the sole exception of *mārga* are to be regarded as defiled. *Mārgasatya,* along with the three *asaṁskṛtadharma-s,* viz. *Ākāsa*, *Pratisaṅkhyānirodha* and *Apratisankhyānirodha* are to be regarded as *anāsrava,* i.e. undefiled.

But the question is still not settled. Why should all *samskṛtadharma-s* with the exception of *Mārgasatya,* be looked upon as instances of *duḥkha?* It is a fact that some of these *samskrtadharma-s* produce an agreeable feeling in us, and in that case, they cannot be considered to be inimical (*pratikulavedanīya*) to us. why should they be regarded as *duḥkha,* in the face of the uncontradicted experience which shows them to be desirable? In answer, Vasubandhu points out that such an agreeable feeling or pleasure (sukha) is much less as compared to the undesirable feelings that are invariably associated with it. If a heap of *māṣa* grains conains a few *mudga* grains, we usually ignore the latter, and prefer to call it a heap of *māṣa* grains:

एवं तर्हि मार्गोऽपि संस्कारदु:खताप्रसङ्गः, संस्कृतत्वात्? प्रतिकूलं हि दु:खमिति लक्षणात्र मार्गो दु:खम्। न हि तस्योत्पाद आर्याणा प्रतिकूलः, सर्वदु:खक्षयावाहनात्। यदापि ते निर्वाणं शान्ततः पश्यन्ति, तदापि यदेव दु:खतो दृष्टं तस्यैव निरोधं शान्ततः पश्यन्ति, न मार्गस्य। यदापि दु:खमप्यत्रास्ति तस्माद् दु:खमेवार्यसत्यमुच्यते, सुखस्याल्पत्वात्, मुद्गादिभावेऽपि माषराश्यादेशवदित्येके। को हि विद्वान् परिषेकसुखाणुकेन गण्डसुखमिति व्यवस्येत्। (*Abhidharmakośa* with *Bhāṣya* and *Sphuṭārthā*, Vol. III, pp. 877-878).

From the expression *eke* employed in this passage, it can be understood that here Vasubandhu is quoting the opinion of some earlier author with whom he is not in complete agreement. From the *Sphuṭārthā* of Yaśomitra, we learn that here Vasubandhu is referring to the view of Bhadanta Kumāralāta, the well-known Sautrāntika teacher, who composed *Kalpanamaṇḍitika dṛṣṭāntapaṅkti,* fragments of which were deciphered and edited by Hermann Lūders. Vasubandhu has quoted here a verse from Kumārlātas' lost work *Duḥkhasaptati,* where several arguments in favour of regarding even pleasure as an instance of *duḥkha* have been summed up. First, the pleasant experience, being associated with some *Karma* that would produce *duḥkha* in the future, can be regarded as the casue of *duḥkha*. In common parlance, we often apply the term denoting the effect to the cause of that effect, albeit in a secondary sense - this is known as *Kāraṇe Kāryopacāraḥ* - the standard examples being "*annṃprāṇāḥ*" and "*āyur vai ghṛtam*". Following this convention, the term *duḥkha* can be appied to *sukha*. Second, as we have already noted, a little pleasure is mixed up with a lot of pain and suffering, and being thus almost insignificant as compared to pain and sorrow, pleasure may very well be ignored or overlooked. Finally, pleasure appears to be desirable only in contrast with pain. In the absence of disagreeable feelings, agreeable feelings lose their charm, and cease to be the objects that we may strive for. That which literally derives its nature from pain and sorrow is also inextricably bound up with pain and sorrow, and thus, they too should be regarded by a wise man as entities to be rejected or avoided. A food mixed with honey and deadly poison may be palatable when we taste it, but its consequences are terrible, and no sensible person would knowingly eat such food:

आह खल्वपि–

दुःखस्य च हेतुत्वात् दुःखैश्चानल्पकैः समुदितत्वात्। दुःखे सति च तदिष्टेर्दुःखमिति सुखं व्यवस्यन्ति।। सहैव तु सुखेन सर्वं भवमार्या दुःखतः पश्यन्ति, संस्कारदुःखैकरसत्वात्। अतो दुःखमेवार्यसत्यं व्यवस्थाप्यते, न सुखम्। कथमिदानीं सुख स्वभावां वेदनां दुःखतः पश्यन्ति? अनित्यतया प्रतिकूलत्वात्। यथा रूपसंज्ञादीन्यपि दुःखतः पश्यन्ति। न च तान्येवं दुःखानि, यथा दुःखा वेदनेति। (*Ibid*, pp. 878-879)

(The last argument of Bhadanta Kumāralāta reminds us of a beautiful verse put in the mouth of Cārudatta by Śudraka in his *Mṛcchakaṭika*:

सुखं हि दुःखान्यनुभूय शोभते घनान्धकारेष्विव दीपदर्शनम्।

सुखात् तु यो याति नरो दरिद्रतां धृतः शरीरेण मृतः स जीवति।।

As we have said before, the expression *eke* employed by Vasubandhu in the course of stating this view indicates that he is not in complete agreement with this view. We now propose to state his criticism against this view of Bhadanta Kumāralāta. The first argument employed by Bhadanta Kumāralāta was that since pleasant feelings are the causes of subsequent sufferings, the former should also be considered to be cases of suffering. Vasubandhu finds several faults with this argument. If something is treated as suffering on the sole ground that it is the cause of some suffering, then *Duhkhasatya* would have only *samudayākara*, and not *duḥkhākāra,* because what is intrinsically a case of suffering is also capable of being casually related to other sufferings. Moreover, the aspirants who have attained the state of

Anāgāmin would not consider the *skandhas* in the Rūpadhātu and Arūpadhātu as instances of suffering, because in their case, such entities would not produce any future sufferings. Thirdly, the mention of *Saṁskāraduḥkhata* in the scriptures would become completely redundant, because if pleasure can be regarded as suffering simply because it produces suffering, there is no further necessity of regarding pleasure as a case of suffering on the ground that it is something produced by causes and conditions, i.e. on such an interpretation, the very concept of *Saṁskāraduhkhatā* becomes redundant. Nor can one save the situation by pointing out that all *saṃskāra-s* are non-eternal or transitory, and hence they are instances of suffering; because in that case, there would be no valid distinction between *duḥkhākāra* and *anityākāra*. But a proper interpretation of *Duḥkhasatya* must be capable of accommodating all the four aspects or *ākāra-s* of *Duḥkhasatya*, viz. *duḥkhākāra, anityākāra, anātmākāra* and *śūnyākāra*. The same entity is treated as suffering from the aspect of *duḥkhākāra* in so far as they are disagreeable to us, just as the same entity is treated as suffering from the aspect of *anityākāra* in so far as it is subject to origination and destruction. We cannot equate *duḥkhākāra* and *anityākāra* simply on the ground that they are equally applicable to the selfsame group of entities; nor can we say on this ground that one of them is rendered redundant by the other. The same planet Venus can be correctly described both as the morning star and the evening star, but this does not entitle us to treat the property of being the morning star as identical with the property of being the evening star, nor can we say that one of these properties is rendered to be redundant by the other. Or, to take an even better example, consider the set of all equilateral triangles, and the set of all equiangular triangles.It can be proved that these two sets are identical. But that would not prove that the concept of equiangularity is identical with the concept of equilaterality - nor would it show that any one of these concepts is redundant.

Vasubandhu maintains that all these four *ākāra-s* provide us with *independent* grounds for treating something as a case of *duḥkha*, and as a matter of fact, it is not a fact that they are equiextensional, i.e. equally applicable to the some set of object. *Duḥkhaduḥkhatā* is applicable only to those things that are intrinsically *(svarūpataḥ)* cases of suffering. The three other *ākāra-s* have a wider applicability. When we notice the impermanence of an entity, a reflection on its nature reveals the fact that it is also disagreeable and hence, a case of suffering. The relevant passages of *Abhidharmakośabhāṣya* are as follows :

यस्तु मन्यते– दुःखहेतुत्वादिति। तस्यासौ समुदयाकारः स्यान्न दुःखाकारः। आर्याणां च रूपारूप्योपपत्रौ कथं दुःखसंज्ञा प्रवर्तते? न हि तेषां दुःख वेदनाहेतुः स्कन्धा भवन्ति। संस्कारदुःखता च सूत्रे किमर्थमुक्ता भवेत्?

यदि तर्ह्यनित्यत्वात् दुःखतः पश्यन्ति, अनित्यदुः खाकारयोः कः प्रतिविशेषः? उदय व्ययधर्मित्वाद नित्यं पश्यन्ति, यथा प्रतिकूलत्वाद् दुःखम्। अनित्यं तु दृश्यमानं प्रतिकूलं भवतीत्य नित्याकारो दुःखा कारमाकर्षति।

(*Abhidharmakośa* with *Bhāṣya* and *Sphuṭārthā*, Vol. III, p. 879)

Vasubandhu now turns to another possible and radical objection his own postion. Vasubandhu's arguments presuppose that there are cases of pleasant feelings, which are not intrinsically intances of suffering. But such a claim can be challenged, and as a matter of fact, Bhadanta Śrīlāta, a pre - Vasubandhu Sautrāntika teacher, had actually adopted such a standpoint. In his opinion, there are no pleasant feelings. He had also adduced scriptural passages and some arguments in favour of his thesis. The scriptural passages cited by him are "यत्किञ्चिद्वेदितमिदमत्र दुःखस्य" "सुखा वेदना दुःखतो द्रष्टव्या," and "दुःखे सुखमिति संज्ञाविर्यासः", which apparently declare that (i) whatever we experience is painful, (ii) the (so-called) pleasant feelings should be regarded as instances of suffering, and (iii) through a mistaken notion, instances of suffering are regarded as instances of pleasure. There are also three arguments in favour of this denial of pleasure as a fact or item of experience. The first one points out that we cannot determine with certainty the causal factors that can produce pleasure. If pleasure is a real entity then it should be produced by some definite factors. But there are no such causal factors, i.e. there is no regular correlation between such supposed causes of pleasure and pleasure itself. An increase in the amount or intensity of the cause is supposed to produce a conrresponding increase or intensity in the effect. Palatable food and drink is supposed to produce pleasure, but when consumed in excessive quantities, they cause discomfort or disease. The sound of music is supposed to be pleasant, but if it is amplified beyond a certain limit, it becomes ear-splitting and causes only annoyance. Pleasure cannot thus be said to have any definite cause, and for the Buddhists (especially Santrāntikas, who do not believe in *Asaṃskṛta dharma-s*), an uncaused entity is as unreal as a square circle. A better conclusion that follows from these examples is that the supposed causes of pleasure are actually causes of suffering. That is why an increase in the amount or intensity of these causes produce suffering that become mainfest, even though they were only latent when the causes were not excessive. Moreover, we often employ the term happiness or 'pleasure' to denote a state where some sort of suffering has merely ceased to exist. Thus, when a severe headache or toothache subsides after the administration of proper medicine, people feel relief, and say - "Now that the pain is gone, I feel happy again". Thus, 'pleasure' here does not stand for any positive entity, it is merely the absence or removal of pain, which happens to be a negative entity. Likewise, when affllicted by hunger or thirst, people feel unhappy, and one afflicted by excessive cold and heat suffer. They feel pleasure when hunger or thirst is removed by the intance of food and drink, or when suffering due to excessive cold or heat is removed by sitting near a blazing fire or by bathing in cold water, as the case may be. Thus, pleasure is never felt, unless it is associated with pain and suffering; and whatever is inextricably bound up with pain and suffering should be considered to be pain or suffering in itself. Finally, people also seem to experience pleasure when one suffering is replaced by another suffering. For example, when a person carrying a heavy load on one of his shoulders feels pain in that shoulder after some time, he places the selfsame burden on the other shoulder, and he seems to derive pleasure or relief from this. But placement of a burden on the shoulder is to be regarded as a cause of suffering - otherwise the person concerned would not feel pain as a consequence of it. Thus, by moving the burden from one shoulder to the other, he is merely exchanging one suffering for another. Pleasure thus turns out to be suffering in disguise-the so-called therefold division of feelings as pleasant (सुखा वेदना), unpleasant feelings (दु:खा वेदना) and indifferent feelings (अदु:खासुखा वेदना) is not tenable.

(See *Abhidharmakośabhāṣya,* Vol. III, p. 880).

Vasubandhu has refuted all these arguments. So far as the scriptural passages or *Buddhavacana-s* are concerned, he shows that Bhadanta Śrīlāta and his followers have misconstrued them, and the independent arguments in favour of their thesis that there is no pleasure or happiness cannot withstand critical examination. So far as the arguments are concerned, let us start examining them, after putting a counter-question; what do Bhadanta Śrīlata and his followers, who deny the very existence of pleasure (*suschāpavādī*) mean by the word 'suffering'? If they say that it is something inimical (*bādhanātmaka*), then the further question arises - why is it considered to be inimical? If it is said in answer that they are inimical in so far as they affect us adversely (*upaghātaka*), then it would follow by parity of reasoning that whatever is felt to be favourable or conducive to our welfare (*anugrahaka*) should be regarded as pleasure or happiness, the fact that noble ones look upon them as suffering is to be explained in a different manner. Due to the impermanence (*anityatā*) or the fact of being conditioned (*saṃskṛta*), these are looked upon as suffering by the noble ones. But this does not detract from the fact that these pleasant feelings are not intrinsically of the nature of suffering. This plenomenological analysis of pleasure is followed by a refutation of the arguments advanced by Śrīlāta.

The first argument of Śrīlāta, viz. there is no dfinite cause of pleasure, rests on the wrong assumption that the object producing pleasure is the *sole* cause of pleasure. Depending on the psychophysical conditions of a person, an object may produce pleasure or pain. When we take all the relevant factors into account, we are in a position to correlate pleasure and pain with their respective causes. No effect is produced by a single cause. Thus, the first argument of Śrīlata, being based on a wrong assumption, stands rejected. Further, if we turn this argument of Śrīlāta on its head, then we might as well argue that suffering also does not have any definite cause, and hence, suffering is unreal or non-existent:

So far as the second argument (viz. 'pleasure' is applicable to removal of pain or suffering) is concerned, we may reasonably ask - when we experience a fragrant smell, or taste a sweet fruit, we experience pleasure as a consequence. There is no rule that such experiences *must* be preceded by unpleasant sensations. Thus, the view which equates pleasure with the mere removal of suffering is not tenable.

So far as the third argument is concerned, one can point out that when the person bearing a load places the burden from one shoulder to the other, there is certainly a change in his physical condition, and that may very well be regarded as the emergence of pleasure. Had the so-called pleasure been identical with the mere replacement of one pain by another, the person concerned would have experienced gradual increase in his sensation of pleasure. This, however, is not the case. Besides, just as the sweet taste of grape juice turns sour when it undergoes fermentation, a pleasant feeling may be followed by an unpleasant feeling. No sensible person would say that since the grape juice turns sour after some duration, it is not sweet at all. Likewise, the denial of pleasure or the ground that it yields place to suffering is not convincing. Thus, the admission of *Duhkhasatya* should not, and cannot be regarded as a doctrine that denies the very existence of pleasure.

(See *Ibid.*, pp. 880-886)

Suffering : An Analytical Study

8

Pradyumna Dube

The Buddha summed up his teachings in his first sermon, which he gave to his five disciples (Pañcavaggiyā bhikkhū)[1] at Benaras soon after he attained enlightenment. It is clear from it that the Buddha had no idea of teaching any philosophical system. His main purpose was to explain to the persons the art of living and to make them free from suffering and all kinds of delusion. He explained the essential doctrines of true religion (Saddhamma). During the Buddha's time many teachers were roaming about the country and they were discussing various philosophical problems. The solution which one teacher offered for the enigmas of life was not accepted by another teacher. The Buddha realised the futility of depending on philosophical speculations for solving the problems of life. So, he firmly opposed and refuted the vain discussions regarding the problems of life. He accepted the world as he found it. He did not require to know how it arose and whence it came. He devoted himself to the work of elucidation of the causes of man's unhappiness and pointing out the practical means for attaining the blissfulness of Nirvāṇa or deliverance from sorrow. He says, "As the vast ocean is impregnated with one taste, the taste of salt, so also my disciples, this law and doctrine is impregnated with one taste, the taste of deliverance.[2]

The doctrine of the Buddha can be discussed under four heads. 1.The existence of suffering, 2 the origin of suffering, 3. the cessation of suffering and 4. the path leading to the cessation of suffering. Here, I am concerned with the first doctrine.

The Existence of Suffering

Suffering is the lot of all human beings. The main concern of religion is removal of suffering and the Buddha confined himself to root out this main problem. He said that one thing he taught was sorrow and the end of sorrow[3]. Suffering is ubiquitous. Unless one knows the right way of living, his life would be an unending stream of suffering, relieved by brief intervals of pleasure which also inevitably end in suffering and boredom. He said." Birth is suffering, old age is suffering, death is suffering, association with the unpleasant is suffering, separation from the pleasant is suffering and not to get what one wants is suffering. In brief, the factors of the five fold clinging to existence are suffering."[4]

The term suffering includes all kinds of evils and dissatisfactions, which affect the life of an average human being. It should not be understood that all beings are equally subject to the same measure of suffering or that all kinds of sufferings are self-infected sufferings. There is no doubt that some sufferings are caused by physical causes or by other living beings and they fall upon saints and sinners alike. If there is an earthquake all are seemingly liable to suffer without any discrimination and all men irrespective of being good or bad are liable to be attacked by wild beasts or by wild men. Undoubtedly, a saint has a greater power of endurance and patience than a common man; so when he is faced with troubles, he can bear them with calm heroism and unperturbed forbearance. But it is a fact that most of the troubles from which people suffer are the creation of their own minds. They arise from worry and anxiety, from anger, malice and envy, from avarice, pride and other undesirable mental status or, as the Buddha used to say, from the cravings, hatreds and infatuations of life.

In modern times, it is often assumed that with the betterment of social and economic conditions, the causes of the unhappiness of man would disappear. The idea behind this thinking is that we are unhappy because we are poor. If mankind were provided with all comforts and amenities of life, it would achieve happiness. But the fact is that many persons, inspite of being rich, are not happy. It means the assumption of happiness on the basis of wealth is wrong. Apart from a sense of economic security, that a thorough tranformation in human nature is also essential in order to achieve happiness, is a truth which every person should accept. True religion aims at the radical transformation of man.

Most of us are unhappy in our lives, because we do not know the true art of living. Undoubtedly, some persons are happier than others. Most probably, they have picked up some of the elements of right living and for that reason their lives have greater significance and joyfulness than is the case with other people. Most of us have become immunized by frequent exposure to unhappy experiences, so that we take our daily sorrows and sufferings as a matter of course. Many of us bear our load of sorrow in the hope that tomorrow will bring us the complete satisfaction of our heart's desire and so we go on without realizing that it is possible for mankind to live at a higher level of existence than the one to which they are normally accustomed. We desire in various ways to forget the time of our sorrows, boredoms and dissatsfactions. The so-called pleasures of life provide a stimulating dose. As a drunkard or a drug addict cannot do without his daily dose of alcohol or morphia, so we all have to fall back, from time to time, upon various mechanical diversions and sensual pleasures to keep ourselves going. After all, as we know, this is not a satisfying mode of living.

It is to be noted that the Buddha has over-drawn the pessimistic view of life. "What think ye", he once asked his disciples, "which is more, the water which is in the four great oceans or the tears which have flown from you and have been shed by you, while you strayed and wandered on the long pilgrimage and sorrowed and wept over a mother's death, a brother's death, the loss of relations, the loss of property, all this you experienced through long ages....[5] The fear of death and decay is always there to make a person pause, while he is engrossed in all sorts of pleasures. This insistence on the sorrows of life is not peculiar to Buddhism.

Pessimism is a mental attitude, which like optimism, is built up in course of one's life-time as a consequence of one's peculiar experiences and his reactions to them. Congenital factors may have something to do with it, but to a large extent, it is an acquired attitude. In the case of the Buddha, the tendency to lay an exaggerated emphasis on the sorrows of life may be traced to the kind of influences to which he was subjected in the early period of his life. His father lived to keep him away from contacts with the ills of life. Siddhārtha had so great a surfeit of sense pleasures that he had no charm in them. These sensual pleasures became for him sources of miseries. Happy and unhappy experiences make a wholesome combination and impart a balanced view of life. There is no wonder if Buddha, as a consequence of the hut-house life to which he lived through childhood and youth, developed a sombre and melancholy attitude towards life.

It is an accepted fact that sufferings and sorrows produce melancholia in the lives of most of us and if some people are happier than others, it is mostly due to the fact that their life is rich in those factors which on the whole make for happiness. The Buddha's aim was to reveal the secret of a truly happy life for mankind. In our life, optimism and pessimism go side by side. This is the position in the cases of pains and pleasures also. It is always wise to see things as they are and not simply to live in a fool's paradise by shutting out the unpleasant aspects of life from consciousness. It is wrong to call Buddhism a pessimistic doctrine, because it does not only emphasize the omnipresence of suffering and its cause in the form of desires, but it points out the way to deliverance from the sorrows of life. It gives to all persons real happiness. In this way, if the starting point in Buddhism is pessimistic and melancholic, it ends as optimistic.

The Doctrine of impermanence

According to Buddhism, the fact of suffering is closely associated with the impermanent nature of things. Whatever is impermanent, is suffering.[6] In our experience, we find nothing as permanent and above change. No object is the same this moment, what it was at the previous moment. All existence is momentary. Due to the limitations of our sense organs we may not be able to perceive the changes which take place from moment to moment, but the change is taking place all the time. There is no halting place, no moment of stability in the uninterrupted stream of change. "Even the ever-lasting hills are slowly being worn away, and every particle of the human body, even the hardest is replaced every seven years. There is no finality or rest within the universe, only ceaseless becoming and a never-ending change."[7] The law of change passes through the four stages of birth, decay, stability and death.[8] It is applicable to all compounded things including man-made objects, ideas and institutions.

Suffering is the consequence of creating bonds of attachment with the transitory things of the world. Whatever is transitory, is painful. Objects are not lost; the germ of dissolution is in each one of them. Our bodies, our possessions, our relations and our experiences-both pleasant and unpleasant-are all transitory in nature. We treat them as if they are everlasting and, when any one of them is dissolved, we lament as if something extraordinary has happened.

It is most important that we should undoubtedly understand the impermanence of everything in the universe. What we call our self, is also subject to the law of impermanence. According to the Buddha, a human being consists of five aggregates and they are all imparmanent[9] and nonsubstantial. The five khandhas or constituents of personality are regarded as impermanent in character. We know that the body is born at a certain time and goes through the processes of growth, decay, old age and death. In the same way, the mental processes appear and disappear. As a matter of fact, the changes in one's mental states become so rapid that they cannot be noticed. This is why a simile can not be given regarding the rapid changeability of consciousnesss.[10]

Thus, it is clear that according to Budhism nothing is permanent, either in nature or in the mind of man. Everything passes away. Some events in life bring us happiness while certain things are a source of pleasure to us. We wish that they should continue as they are and should not change, but when they are changed and become non-existent we find ourselves in the grip of sorrow. In this way, impermanence is the cause of suffering.

Theory of Anatta

There is a deep relation between suffering and anatta.[11] The question, 'what am I?, drew the attention of the sages of the Upaniṣads. When a group of thirty gentle persons came to the Buddha to enquire from him whether he had seen a woman who had run away from them. He replied by asking them, "Which is of greater importance young men, to search for the woman or for your I?"[12] But the method of enquiry about "I" was slightly different from that of the sages of the Upanisads. He did not try to understand "I" direct, but he adapted an indirect method to understand what was not the self. This is known as the Anatta doctrine of Buddhism. According to the criterion laid down by the Buddha, what was ephemeral and perishable could not be the self. On the basis of this, he came to the conclusion that mental aggregates, whether taken individually or collectively, could not be regarded as self or a part of the self. The Buddha says in one place-"Wherefore, monks, whatsoever there is of body, whatsoever there is of sensations, whatsoever there is of perception, whatsoever there is of thinking, whatsoever there is of consciousness in the past, in the future and at the present moment......gross or subtle, mean or exalted, remote or close at hand.....in the light of highest wisdom, is to be regarded thus "This belongs not to me, this, am I not, this is not myself."[13] According to the Buddha what belongs to me should be quite under my control and I should be able to do whatever I like it. We are not in a position to say, "Let my body be thus, let not my body be so." Similarly our sersations, our feelings, ideas, volition and consciousness are not under our control. Hence, they cannot singly or together be regarded as my 'Self'. The theory of Anatta has been explained in Milindapañho through the dialogue between Milinda and Nāgasena. As conclusion, in the end of the dialogue, it has been said that really there does nct exist soul.[14] What is anatta, is suffering. It has been already explained.

A lot of material on suffeing is available in Pāli and Buddhist literature. Keeping in mind the limitation of time I have not discussed it at length.

References

1. Pañcavaggiyā bhikkhū are—Aññākoṇḍañña, Vappa, Bhaddiya, Mahānāma and Assaji, See Mahāvaggo (M.V.). edited by Bhikkhu J. Kashyap, Nava Nalanda Mahavihar, Nalanda, 1980, pp.15-16.
2. Seyyathāpi, Bhikkave, Mahāsamuddo ekaraso loṇaraso, evameva khobhikkhave, ayaṃ dhammavinayo ekaraso vimuttiraso. Cullavaggo 9.2.3, edited by Bhikkhu J.Kashyap, Pāli Publication Board (Bihar Government), 1956, p.357.

3. Pubbe cāham bhikkave, etarhi ca dukkhuṃ cava paññapemi, dukkhassa ca nirodhaṃ. Alagaddūpama Sutta, Majjhima Nikāya (M.N.) Volume (Vol.)1, edited by Bhikkhu J.Kashyap, Pali Publication Board (Bihar Government),1958, p. 185.

4. Idaṃ kho pana, bhikkave, dukkhaṃ ariyasaccaṃ. Jāti pi dukkhāṁ jarā pi dukkhā, vyādhi pi dukkho, maraṇaṃ pi dukkam appiyehi sampayogo dukkho, piyahi vippayogo dukkho, yaṃ picchaṃ na labhati taṃ pi dukkhaṃ. Saṃkhittena pañcupādānakkhanadhā dukkhā Dhammacakkappavattanaṃ, M.V.,p.13.

5. Taṃ kim maññattha, bhikkave, kataṃ nu kho bahutaraṃ yam vā dighena addhunā sandhavataṃ sansarataṃ amanāpasaṃpayogā manāpavippayogā kandantānaṃ rodantānaṃ assu passannaṃ paggharitaṃ yaṃ vā catūṣu mahāsamuddsu udakam ti?

   "Yatahā kho mayaṃ ...., Mātumaranaṃ paccanubhontānaṃ ...rodantānaṃ assupassannaṃ paggharitaṃ...... pitumaraṇaṃ ....natveva catūsu mahasamuddesu udakaṃ. Assusutta, Saṃyutta Nikāya (S.N.), Vol. Il, edited by Bhikkhu J. Kashyap, Pāli Publication Board (Bihar Government), 1959,p.152.

6. "Yaṃ Panāniccaṃ dukkhaṃ vā taṃ sukhaṃ vā ti"? "Dukkhaṃ, bhanteti". M.N. Vol.1,p.183; Yadāniccaṃ taṃ dukkhaṃ. S.N., Vol.ll,p. 259.

7. Humphery's Christian: Buddhism, p.80 quoted in Bahadur Mal: *The Religion of the Buddha & its Relation to Upaniṣadic Thought* (Rel.B.R.U.T.),Hoshiarpur, 1958,p.89.

8. Lakṣaṇāni punarjātirjarā sthitiranityatā. Abhidharmakośa (A.k.) 245 ga-gha (3rd and 4th foot of the Kārikā); Tatra jātistaṃ dharmaṃ janayati, sthitiḥ sthāpayati, jarā jarayati, anityatā vināśayati.Abhidharmakośabhāṣya (A.K.B.) on 245 ga-gha.

9. Rūpam, bhikkhave, aniccaṃ vedanā aniccā, saññā aniccā, saṅkhārā aniccā, viññāṇaṃaniccaṃ. M.N.Vol. II,p. 258.

10. "Nāhaṃ, bhikkhave, aññaṃ ekadhammaṃ pi samanupassāmi yaṃ evaṃ lahuparivattaṃ yathayidaṃ cittaṃ. Yāvañcidaṃ, bhikkhave, upamā pi na sukarā yāva lahuparivattaṃ cittam" ti. Aṅguttara Nikāya (A.N.), Vol.I, edited by Bhikkhu J. Kashyap, Pāli Publication Board (Bihar Government), 1960, p. 10.

11. Yadaniccaṃ taṃ dukkhaṃ; *Yam dukkham tadanattā*; yadanattā taṃ 'netaṃ mam, nesohamasmi, na meso attā'ti evametaṃ yathābhūtaṃ sampaññāyā daṭṭabbaṃ. S.N. Vol. II-III, P. 259.

12. Taṃ kiṃ maññatha vo,kumārā, kataṃ nu kho tumhākhaṃ varaṃ yaṃ vā tumhe itthiṃ gaveseyyātha, yaṃ vā attānaṃ gaveseyyāthā ti ? M.V., p.25.

13. Tasmātiha, Bhikkhave. yaṃ kiñci rūpaṃ atītānāgatapaccuppannaṃ, ajjhattaṃ vā bahiddhā vā, olārikaṃ vā sukhumaṃ vā, hīnaṃ vā panītam vā, yaṃ dūre santike vā sabbaṃ rūpam 'netaṃ mama, nesohamasmi, na meso attā'ti-evametaṃ yathābhūtaṃ sampaññāya daṭṭhabbaṃ. Yā kāci vedanā ...pe .....yā kāci saññā ....ye keci saṃkhārā ... yaṃ kiñci viññāṇaṃ atītānāgatapaccuppannaṃ, ajjhattaṃ vā bahiddhā vā olārikaṃ vā sukhamaṃ vā, hīnaṃ vā paṇītaṃ vā yaṃ dūre santike vā, sabbaṃ viññānaṃ 'netaṃ mama, nesohamasim, na meso attā'ti - evametaṃ yathābhūtaṃ sampaññāya daṭṭhabbaṃ. M.N.Vol.1, p. 184.

14. Paramattahato panettha pugglo nūpalabbhati. *Milindapañho,* edited by Swami Dwarika Das Sastri, Bauddh Bharati, Varanasi, 1979, p. 21.

Buddha's Altruism

9

Angraj Chaudhary

The ubiquitous nature of the noble truth of suffering based on the Buddha's observation is an undeniable fact of human life. No philosopher worth the name has ever contradicted it. All six systems of Indian philosophy have accepted it as an incontrovertible fact of life. As far as the Buddha is concerned, he propounds his philosophy when he analyses the causes of suffering. This philosophy, like most of the philosophies of the world, is not an outcome of his thinking but is a direct product of his experiential wisdom. By practising vipassana meditation which he himself discovered, he found out the causes of suffering. Suffering does not come from outside, it comes from within. It is not caused by any outside force nor is it caused fortuitously, nor is it caused by any god but it is caused by one's own self by the internal dynamics of one's mind. We are the makers of our suffering.

He then explained at great length that our suffering is caused by our cravings and aversions, and these arise due to our ignorance of the real nature of things. By walking on the eightfold path consisting of sila samadhi and panna he attained wisdom in the light of which he saw that all mundane things are impermanent and so it is not wise to hanker after them, and consequently multiply our suffering and keep on moving endlessly in the cycle of birth and death and suffer incalculably. How did the Buddha come to this conclusion ? Not by logic and intellect but by his experiential wisdom which he attained by practising vipassana meditation.

His practice of vipassana meditation led him to the conclusion that as we cause our own suffering so we can ourselves put an end to it. How ? By removing the causes of suffering. And how to remove the causes of suffering ? By observing the precepts, practising meditation and attaining wisdom the Buddha came to this conclusion by walking on the eightfold path. It will not therefore be incorrect to say that the Buddha's philosophy has an in-built action plan. He himself walked on the eightfold path and saw that our suffering is caused by the mental defilements of craving and aversion which arise in ignorance and he also saw that it can be annihilated by our ethical and moral actions which are performed to remove the defilements responsible for our suffering. In conclusion he said that it is our impure mind that causes our suffering and to get rid of it is to purify our mind. Thus in the teachings of the Buddha which are out-and-out pragmatic and realistic we find a happy combination of philosophy, psychology and ethics. Here is an in-depth study of the psychology of the mind the dynamics of which makes us suffer, an in-depth study of philosophy which explains the cause of our suffering as also an in-depth study of ethics which explains what the impurities of the mind are and how they can be removed. We observe ethical precepts and concentrate our mind and with this mind we see the reality as it is. If we want to harvest a good crop of peace and happiness we have to weed out our mind, otherwise there will be a luxuriant growth of weeds as a result of which all prospective plants of peace and happiness will be choked and smothered. What is actually needed for extirpating suffering is to change the dynamics of our mind. The dynamo that produces desires is also fuelled by the desires. In order to stop this dynamo from going on and on we have to stop fuelling it, which means we have to eliminate our desires. This understanding of the rise of the desires also includes the understanding of the stopping of desires. An impure and defiled mind is the spring of the desires. If our mind is made pure and free of defilements the spring of the desires will dry up.

The Buddha was not a pessimist as many have made him out to be. In fact, the charge of pessimism has been laid at his door by several critics. But this is not tenable. The incomparable physician that he was, he diagnosed the disease thoroughly and prescribed the medicine to get rid of it for good. How can such a philosopher be called a pessimist ? As he understood that man's mind is the spring of all his actions it is incumbent, he said, on man to purify it, and for purifying it he has to walk on the eightfold path. To walk wisely on this path man has to attain the knowledge of reality, has to eliminate his desires and has to work hard without ever being unmindful.

So when he asked his monks to go forth for the good and welfare of many, what he meant was going to the people, teaching them the way to put an end to their suffering by walking on the eightfold path of sila samadhi and panna. Why did he ask the monks to go alone and not in a group ? There are, to my mind, two reasons for it. One was that a monk is supposed to live a lonely life which is conducive to his practice of sadhana, and the second reason was that in those days monks were few and suffering people were many. It was necessary for all people to listen to the teachings of the Buddha. How was it possible ? So the Buddha thought to let one monk go to a particular area and be with the people of that place. A monk would be able to preach the Dhamma to a large number of people. At least one enlightened person would be there where there was none. So if the monks went to different places singly so many areas would be covered and in fact there would be many islands in the deep wide sea of misery. As Shelly says — 'Many a green isle needs there must be, In this deep wide sea of misery'. With this end in view he exhorted the monks to go forth alone 'for the gain of many, for the welfare of many with compassion for men and gods alike'.

'Bahujana hitaya, bahujana sukhaya' obviously means that the Buddha's mission was to help people out of their suffering. So if some people think there is a contradiction between the Buddha's propounding of Dukkham ariyasaccam — the first noble truth and his mission to take measures to put an end to suffering, I am afraid, they have not understood the spirit of the Buddha's teachings. He propounded the first noble truth of suffering all right but he never said that suffering can never end. In fact, he said out of personal experience that, if the cause of suffering is rooted out, it is bound to end. So where is the contradiction ? Where is the paradox ? When he exhorted the monks to go forth and work for the gain of many and for the welfare of many, it is quite in keeping with his mission as also with his compassionate nature.

The Buddha and his disciples did not only teach people to walk on the eightfold path and work out their salvation. Of course, it was the most important thing for them to do. But the Buddha and his disciples did not only put a premium on their spiritual welfare but they also took great care of their material happiness and well-being.

I think one would be justified to say that the Buddha's concern was both, material as well as spiritual. We do not see him neglecting our material well-being. But definitely the balance seems to dip in favour of the spiritual well-being of the people. If the highest spiritual well-being is achieved, the material well-being will take care of itself. That is why we see the Buddha teaching so many persons and taking them out of their misery. The Buddha goes to the thief Angulimala to save him from going to hell. He taught him the Dhamma which changed the course of his life. From a fearful robber he became an arhat. He explains to Kasibharadwaja that his agricultural produce pales into insignificance in comparison to his produce which unlike Kasibharadwaja's produce allays the hunger for good. In his agricultural operation faith is the seed and austerity, rain. He makes it clear to Dhaniya that material comforts cannot cpmpare with the nibbanic peace that a samana attains. He explains to so many Brahamanas the quintessence of Dhamma. In the Canki sutta it is made clear how one can find out what Dhamma is. He was so compassionate that when his mahaparinibbana was nearing he gave his teachings to a wanderer named Subhadda. Thus he quenched the spiritual thirst of that man. The compassionate nature of the Buddha and his altruistic attitude to help the needy is clear from what he says to Ananda who does not allow Subhadda to visit the Buddha anticipating trouble from him. 'Ananda, do not prevent him from coming to me. Whatever Subhadda will ask me (*yam kinci mam Subhaddo pucchissati*) it will be with a view to knowing the highest truth (*sabbam tam annapaekkhova pucchissati*) and not with a desire to give me trouble (*no vihesapekkho*).' Such examples can be multiplied *ad libitum*. His objective was to teach them the noble eightfold path and exhort them to walk on it to end their suffering and break the cycle of birth and death. This is how one can get rid of suffering for ever. To this end he kept on working ceaselessly. Except the time when he ate, drank and slept and except when he answered the call of nature he kept on preaching. *'Annatra aitapitakhayitasayita, annatra uccarapassavakamma, annatra niddakilamathavinodana apariyadinnayevassa, Sariputta, Tathagatassa dhammadesana, apariyadinnamyevassa dhammapadabyanjanam, apariyadinnamyevass* Tathagatassa panhapatibhanam. (M.N. Mahasihanda Sutta).

But it is not possible for all to end their suffering and attain nibbana in one life. Most of us have so many deep layers of sankharas that it is not possible to get rid of all of them in one life. It will be several lives before they are all burnt out. But every time we are born we suffer from different kinds of physical ailments and mental afflictions. The Buddha was so compassionate that he did not lose sight of such ailments people suffered from. There are examples in the Tipitaka that the Buddha himself helped his suffering monks. He also asked other monks if they had enough to live by. Like a loving father he saw to it that the monks do not suffer from lack of food and robe and other necessary requisites. Is it not his altruism ? Is he concerned only with his own salvation, only with his own spiritual well-being and not with the needs of others ? Once when he came to know about a sick monk who was not attended to by any, he himself along with Ananda took great care of him. The monk was so weak that he was not able to get up from his bed. He was soiled with his own urine and excreta. The Buddha asked Ananda to fetch hot water. He poured water on his body, cleaned him and made him sleep on a clean bed. He said that the monks must help one another when they are ill, or who will take care of them. The Buddha said that one who serves the sick serves me. *Yo gilanam upatthahati so mam upatthahati.* Is it not a great altruistic thought ? Was it not a great altruistic action of the Buddha ? Does it not show his infinite compassion for suffering humanity ? He equates serving the sick with practising Dhamma.

The altruistic attitude of the Buddha can be seen in what he did for the downtrodden and the oppressed. His Dhamma is not meant only for kings and rich men. He taught his Dhamma to leper

Suppabuddha, to the poor Sopaka who was born in a *candal* family, to the low born Suppiya, to Sunita who was a sweeper. He showered his compassion on a hunter's daughter Capa. He showered it on Ambapali, on Abhaya mata, Padmavati, on Addhakasi, on Vimala who were all sex workers of his times. Once he did not begin to preach because there was a hungry farmer there and only after he was fed he started his preaching. What do all these instances show ? They show that the Buddha was not unaware of the need to ameliorate the conditions of the poor and the neglected.

Although his primary concern was to cross the four floods, eradicate human cravings and attain nibbana, he did not ignore the material well-being of the people. In the *Kutadanta Suttah* it is said that it is the duty of a king to provide seed, agricultural implements and other infrastructure to the farmer. It is also the duty of a king to provide a merchant with the seed money and other necessaries to enable him to set up his business and above all it is also the primary duty of a king to see that no young man and woman remain unemployed. He went on further to say that many evils of society would disappear if the minds of the youth are not empty. An empty mind is the devil's workshop. Besides, if all are fruitfully engaged in their work, society would be free from thieves, dacoits and other perpetrators of crime. This seminal thought of the Buddha goes a long way in making society prosperous, free from crimes and other disturbances and in taking care of the material well-being of the people. The condition of the poor, the needy, the unemployed as also the sick and the neglected sections of society must be ameliorated before peace and harmony in society can be achieved. In the *Cakkavattisihanada Sutta* and the *Agganna Sutta*, it has been shown how man's mind is defiled by craving, aversion and other polluting factors. This analysis has been made so that man can keep himself from these pollutants. This is altruism par excellence.

The four sublime states viz. *metta, karuna, mudita* and *upekkha* can assume significance only in a human society, and each one of the states is the direct product of one's altruistic attitude. When you feel love (*metta*) for the people around, you are taking an active interest in the other. In other words *metta* is *hitesita* (thinking of doing good to others) *anukampa* (compassion) and *abyapado* (absence of hatred), in short it is *hita sukha upanayakamata* – the desire of bringing to one's fellowmen that which is welfare and good, *karuna* is the desire of removing bane and sorrow— ahita dukkhapanaya kamata or it means when your heart is moved to see your fellow beings suffer, *mudita* is sympathetic joy i.e. you feel joy when somebody has made progress and has achieved success and *upekkha* i.e. equanimous attitude and being disinterested in whatever happens to one. The Buddha always practised these *viharas* or at leat one of them. This is perhaps one of the reasons why we find the word '*viharati*' being used in the context of the Buddha. *Ekam samayam Bhagava Buddho Savatthiyam viharati*. When you take active interest in others these sublime states can develop. The Buddha did take active interest in others. So these sublime states are altruistic concepts.

If we read the Jataka stories it will be clear how the Bodhisattva always thinks of the welfare and good of others, how he takes pity on those who are in trouble and how he remains equanimous in adverse situations. Is it not his altruistic activity ? This concept of Bodhisattva became so comprehensive in Mahayana Buddhism that Bodhisattva became the embodiment of Mahakaruna. I have analyzed this concept of Bodhisattva in my paper entitled Acarya Santideva's Humanism.

In short, the Buddha was a pragmatic philosopher who propounded the noble truth of suffering but he always practised the four *Brahmaviharas*, and moved by his desire to help others he practised altruism.

Concept of Suffering from the Bodhisattva Viewpoint of Self-Dedication

10

J. Sitaramamma

From thebeginning of mankind man has been striving hard to make his life happy and avoid suffering(Dukkha). No other thinker was as sensitive as Buddha to the fact of Dukkha (Suffering is of three kinds viz physical, mental and spiritual). Buddha says ; O monks! two things do I teach, Dukkha and the cessation of Dukkha.[1]

1. He could see man experience suffering at every moement of his life. Birth, decay, disease, death, coming into contact with those who are not liked and separation from those who are liked, not to get what one desires are suffering. In short, the five aggregates that conduce to clinging are suffering.[2]
2. In a way the concept of Dukkha in Buddhism is a more comprehensive concept than that of suffering. It includes not merely physical and mental suffering, but also such deeper ideas as imperfection, impermanence, emptiness, conflict, unsubstantiality, unsatisfactoriness and ignorance concerning the true nature of man and his existence. Buddhism speaks of three kinds of Dukkha confronting human existence: namely *Dukkha Dukkhata, Viparinama Dukkhata and Sankhara Dukkhata.*[3]

Meaning of Dukkha (Suffering):

Dukkha in Pali or *Dukkha* in Sanskrit is a compound of two words. 'DU' and 'KHA' the prefix 'DU' is used in the sense of 'vile' (*kucchita*). It signifies something bad, disagreeable, uncomfortable or unfavourable. The suffix 'KHA' is used in the sense of 'empty' (*tuccha*), it signifies emptiness or unreality. Therfore Dukkha stands for something that is vile and imaginary. Buddhaghosa is of the opinion that things that are impermanent, harmful and devoid of substantiality are characterized otherwise by ignorant people and this leads to pain and misery[4]. Hence, these are called Dukkha. In the ordinary sense Dukkha means suffeing, pain, misery or discomfort. It is something which is opposed to happiness, comfort or ease. Dukkha according to the Buddha does not merely refer to the ordinary corporeal suffering of man. Rhys Davids has rightly remarked that it is difficult to find one word which could embrace the whole concept of the term Dukkha as used by the Buddha in his teachings.The words in English are too specialized, limited and strong. The words such as ill, illness, disease are not exact but only half synonyms in this connotation[5]. Dukkha is equally mental and physical pain. It refers more to mental than physical plane, sorrow to the mental plane. But they have been used even in default. Wherein, more rendering was not possible. The words disease, illness, suffering, trouble, misery, distress, agony, affliction, woe, etc., have been used in certain connection though they are never fully right. Rahula is of the opinion that it would be better to leave it untranslated than to give an incomplete and wrong idea by conveniently rendering it as pain or suffering[6]. To quote Chirstmas Humphery: "Dukkha covers all that we understand by pain, illness, disease-physical and mental including such minor forms of discomfort, disharmony, limitations, frictions or in a philosophical sense the awareness of incompleteness or insufficiency"[7].

Stcherbatsky stressing the philosophical implications of Dukkha observes that the Buddha's statements like 'The vision is dukkha' or 'all the elements influenced by *rago*, *doso* and *moho* are dukkha' can be properly understood, if their philosophical sense is taken into consideration[8]. The elements of the world influenced by passions are constantly in a state of flux (*sasravah*). This agitated state of the elements have to be gradually appeased and finally extinguished from the influences of the passions. A state of uniform motion or rest of the elements (*asasravah*) has to be attained.

The cessation of suffering can be brought about by the noble eight-fold path. When the Buddha teaches that craving is at the root of man's suffering, it must be noted that he only suggests that man should liberate himself from craving, and grasping and not of his need. The entire Buddhist philosophy is nothing but an attempt at understanding human suffering and redeeming man from the same. The mind subjected to ignorance is conditioned by the five-fold defilements (*nivaranas*) like the sensual desires (kamacchanda) malevolence (*vyapada*), inactivity and drowsiness (*thinamidda*), flurry and worry (*Unddhacca kukkucca*) doubt and wavering (*vicikiccha*). The Buddha observes that to attain freedom from Dukkha, one has to overcome the five-fold defilements (nivaranas) which have made the mind conditioned and unstable. One attains liberation when one perceives things 'as they really are' and not as they appear to be[9].

The persons who can perceive things as they really are attain Bodhi. One who aims at attaining Buddhattva (Buddhahood) is a Bodhisattva. Therefore in this paper an attempt is made to discuss about the concept of suffering from the Bodhisattva view point of self-dedication.

The Pali term *Bodhisatta* is composed of *Bodhi* which means wisdom or enlightenment and *Satta* which means devoted to or intent on. A Bodhisatta, therefore, means one who is devoted to, or intent on, wisdom, enlightenment[10]. In the Sanskrit Bodhisattva means a being aspiring to become a Buddha or an enlightened being, In Tibetan Buddhism it is translated as "a being with heroic mind"[11]. D.T.Suzuki describes Bodhisattva as an "intellectual being."[12]. L.D.Barnett calls him a "Creature of enlightenment"[13]. Sir Charles Eliot says "Bodhisattva means one whose essence is knowledge[14]. In the early Mahayana, the Bodhisattva occupies a position next to the Buddha. He has all the qualifications to become a Buddha. Later he is regarded as equal to Buddha in many respects.

The Sanskrit term Bodhisattva is the name given to any one who, motivated by great compassion, has generated bodhicitta, which is a spontaneous wish to attain Buddhahood for the benefit of all living beings. The moral discipline of the Bodhisattvas is a higher moral discipline and it is the main path that leads to the ultimate happiness of great enlightenment. In the *Pratimoksha sutra*, the Buddha says that it would be better for us to die than to break our moral discipline because death destroys only this one life, whereas breaking our moral discipline destroys our opportunity to experience happiness in many future lives, and condemns us to experience the sufferings of lower rebirths over and over again.

In *Saddharma Pundarikà Sutra*, it is stated that Avalokiteswara advises Kasyapa in the following manner. 'Just as one worships the new and not the full moon, just so those who believe in me should know the Bodhisattvas and not the Tathagata" or "from the Buddha arises only the disciples and Pratyeka Buddhas" but from the Boddhisattva the perfect Buddha himself is born.

According to Mahayana Buddhism any one who develops *Bodhicitta* is a *Bodhisattva*, i.e. a being destined to attain Bodhi (knowledge) becomes the Buddha in the long run. In fact every Mahayanist is a *Bodhisattva* aiming at Buddhahood. Though the Buddhahood is within his easy reach, Bodhisattva takes the vow that he would postpone his attainment and help the entire world to Nirvana. The Hero of *Vimalakirtinirdesa Sutra*, Vimalakirti says that, "As all other beings are sick, so I am sick, all beings are considered as one."[15]

According to Buddhism there are three types of Bodhisattvas : namely, intellectual Bodhisattvas, devotional Bodhisattvas and energetic Bodhisattvas. The energetic ones always seek opportunities to be of service to others. Nothing gives them greater delight than active service. For them work is happiness and happiness is work[16]. They are not happy unless they are active. As king Sanghabodhi of Sri Lanka said they "bear this body of flesh and blood for the good and happiness of the world". They live not for themselves but for others as well. This spirit of selfless service is one of the chief characteristics of all Bodhisattvas. With relentless energy they work not as slaves but as masters. They crave for neither fame nor name. They are interested only in service. It is immaterial to them whether others recognize their selfless service or not. They are utterly indifferent to praise or blame. They forget themselves in their disinterested service to others. They would sacrifice even life itself could such action save another fellow being.[17] A Bodhisattva who forgets himself in the service of others should practise *Karuna* and *Metta* (Compassion and loving kindness) to an exceptionally high degree. A Bodhisattva desires the good and welfare of the world. "The compassion of a Bodhisattva consists in realizing the equality of oneself with others (*Paratma-Samata*) and also the Substitution of others for oneself (*para-atma-parivartana*)" When he does so he loses his Ī-notion and finds no difference between himself and others. He returns good for evil, and helps even unasked the very persons who have wronged him, for he knows that "the strength of a religious teacher is his patience". "Being reviled, he reviles not, being beaten he beats not, being annoyed he annoys not. His forgiveness is unfailing even as the mother earth suffers in silence all that may be done to her".[17]

It is the aim of a Bodhisattva : "In all lands may all the sufferings of living beings come to an end....may those who suffer hunger and thirst receive food and drink in abundance...may the blind see, the deaf hear, the woman with child give birth painlessly". He thinks "it is indeed better that I alone suffer than all living beings should reach the abodes of the evil forms of existence"[18] The Bodhisattva proclaims all merit which I have acquired, I here without concern give up for the welfare of all living beings".[19] In Mahayana the sublimest religious ideal, that of absolute altruism, is conjoined with the realisation of the profoundest metaphysical truth, that of *Anatta* or no-self.The Bodhisattva of the Mahayana represents not the mere juxtaposition but the living spiritual unity of these two basic themes of Buddhism.[20]

It is unanimously agreed that to remove one's own pain does not in itself count as moral act, while to soothe the pains of others would in general count as engaging in action which is morally virtuous. Santideva argued that no morally significant distinction can be drawn between the two imperatives. It means he acts equally whether it is his pain or others'. Therfore perfect Buddhahood is finally the fulfilment of the moral imperative, the imperative to strive unceasingly to remove the suffering of all sentient beings without discrimination.[21]

According to his reasoning Santideva Says: "I shall call the position that morality requires that if I am to remove my own pain I must (moral imperative) act to remove the pains of others without discrimination, the Universal thesis": Santideva and his commentators want to argue for the Universal thesis based on the rational that because it is pain it is to be removed. It is rational that if it (i.e.my pain) is to be prevented, all (pain) also is to be prevented.[22]

For a real Buddhist there is no such thing as a self. We are each of us an ever-changing composite of various radically impermanent psycho-physical components extended in space and time. But a composite thing itself is a fiction, in itself it is nothing at all. Thus Santideva wants to argue, "we cannot rationally talk of the owner of a pain". It follows that Santideva wants to hold an extreme version of the no-ownership theory for sensations—pains are for him quite literally without owners at all. Since under such circurnstances we cannot refer to the owners of pains, we can refer only to pains. It is not possible to draw a limit to the eradication of just some pains, but one is obliged to eradicate, or strive to eradicate, all pains. Santideva has argued that without selves there are no selves, with no selves there are no persons, and with no persons we cannot distinguish between my pain and your pain. Navertheless, we do as a matter of fact all set out to remove (our own) pains. That is a basic fact of human nature.

To give fearlessness is to protect other living beings from fear or danger. For example, if we rescue someone from a fire or from some other natural disaster, if we protect others from physical violence, or if we save animals and insects who have fallen into water or who are trapped, we are practising giving fearlessness. If we are not able to rescue those in danger,we can still give fearlessness by making prayers and offerings so that they may be released from danger. We can also practise giving fearlessness by praying for others to become free from their delusions, especially the delusion of self-grasping, which is the ultimate source of all fear.

In the *Prajna Paramita sutra*, the Buddha says that the moral discipline of a Bodhisattva does not degenerate if he or she enjoys beautiful forms, sounds, tastes or other objects of the senses, but if a Bodhisattva develops concern for his own walfare, both his moral discipline and his *bodhicitta* degenerate. With the motivation of *bodhicitta* no action can be non-virtuous because *bodhicitta* eliminates self-cherishing, which is the root of all non-virtuous actions. Even if a Bodhisattva has to kill, this action is not non-virtuous because it is performed surely for the benefit of all living beings. Therefore, their *bodhicitta* ensures that all their actions are pure.[23]

In one of his previous births Sakyamuni was still a *bodhisattva*. At that time he was the captain of a ship that was ferrying 500 merchants on a special voyage. With his clairvoyance he saw that one of the merchants was planning to kill all the others. Seeing that as a result of this, the merchant would be reborn in hell, he generated great compassion for him and for his intended victims. He decided to take upon himself the karma of killing rather than allow all 500 merchants to suffer and so, with pure *bodhichitta* motivation, he killed the wicked merchant. In this way he protected that merchant from a hellish rebirth and saved the lives of all the others (As a result of this action of killing,that *Bodhisattva* made great spiritual progress).

The Bodhisattvas practise the moral discipline benefiting living beings and for that cause they may go to any extreme point of suffering. Because his main aim was to do whatever needed to be done to make someone also happy. When others are happy their minds are more open and receptive to advice and example. This is well illustrated by an episode from the life of the great Tibetan Teacher Geshe Langri Tangpa.

A newly delivered woman was frightened that her child would die with sickness like her elder kid. The woman expressed her anxiety to her mother. Her mother gave an advice, based on that she had taken her child to a Bodhisattva who could save her daughter's life. With folded hands she prayed to the bodhisattva to accept her request. For the sake of her daughter's life she announced in a public gathering that 'take care of your child I don't want to keep the baby with me any more; from now onwards it is your responsibility'. Bodhisattva nodded his head. His disciples with an exclamation asked him if she was his daughter, then he said yes. After some time the child had recovered from her sickness and the mother wanted to take away her daughter. The Bodhisattva happily handed over the child to her mother.[24] By knowing the fact that just to protect the child he accepted the lie told by her, his disciples felt themselves ashamed to suspect his teacher and asked for his apology.

In the *Suvarna Prabhasa Sutra* there is an interesting account of a Bodhisattva who out of compassion threw himself before a hungry tigress which had five cubs. According to this account, long ago there lived a king named Maharatha. He had three sons, Mahapranada, Mahadeva and Mahasattavavan. These princes were one day wandering about in a great park and came to a lonely place called "The twelve shrubs". "Mahasattvavan was not disturbed by any fears or misgiving but his brothers were not so brave. Suddenly they saw a tigress in that hollow "The twelve shrubs". She had whelped seven days before, had five cubs, and was emaciated through hunger and thirst. The three brothers talked of her sad plight and said, what can this poor creature eat, Mahasattvavan asked his brother to walk on and said, "I shall go into this hollow to do something." He then uttered these words. "I, moved by compassion, give my body for the good of the world and for the attainment of bodhi." When he threw himself before the tigress, she did not do anything to him. The Bodhisattva understood that she was very weak. He looked round for a weapon, but could find none. He took a strong hundred year old bamboo creeper, cut his throat, and fell dead near the tigress.[25]

The story of King Sibi is found in four different versions in Buddhist Sanskrit literature. It is related in the *Avadana-sataka*, the *Jatakamala* and the *Avadana-kalpalata*.[26] According to the *Avadana-sataka*, King Sibi having distributed all his wealth among the people, thinks of the small insects. He inflicts several wounds on his body with a weapon, and feeds the bees and mosquitoes with his blood, as if they were his children. In the meantime, Sakra, the chief of the devas, assumes the shape of a vulture in order to put King Sibi to test. The king offers the vulture a feast of his own flesh, and tells him to eat as much as he needs. Sakra then appears in the guise of the Hindu priest (Brahmin), and asks for the king's eyes, which are willingly given. Sakra praises and blesses the king for his generosity. In Ksemendra's first story of Sibi, the king feeds an 0gre(raksasa) with his flesh and blood as a recompense for a few beautiful verses, which Indra, disguised as an ogre, recites in his presence. Indra asks him if he felt any pain or grief at the sacrifice of his limbs. Sibi replies in the negative, and says: "If it is true that my mind was not touched by that pain, then may I, by the power of this truthful asseveration, regain my body as it was." His body immediately becomes whole and sound again. It may be stated that this device of *saty-adhisthana* (resolution by truth) is employed by the later Mahayanist writers in order to restore their heroes and heroines to their normal physical condition after the mutilation suffered by them in the exercise of charity. In some stories, Indra, who often appears as the tempter. compensates them at the end by his divine power, but Ksemendra prefers this curious method of *saty-adhisthan* for avoiding a tragic conclusion of the moving tales. The hero cannot be left torn and bleeding after his superhuman sacrifice. This tendency to finish the stories in a happy vein is most marked in Ksemendra's writings, while Sura does not always care to restore his mangled heroes to their pristine strength and beauty. The same King Sibi is also the hero of the second story in Arya Sura's *Jataka-mala*. Sakra, in the guise of a blind priest, asks for the gift of one eye, but the king gives him both eyes; Sibi remains blind for some time, but Sakra restores his eyes to him in the end and bestows on him the power of seeing things at a distance.[27]

Ksemendra also narrates a second story of King Sibi. His capital was called Sikhi-ghosa. When a violent epidemic raged in the country, the physicians declared that the sick could be cured only by drinking the blood of a man, who had always practised forbearance since the day of birth. The King knew that he had never yielded to anger, and that his mother had also completely eschewed it during the pre-natal period. He gave his blood to the sick during six months.

The story of Rukmavati is told in the *Divy-avadana* and the *Avadana-kalpa-lata*.[28] She is a charitable lady of the town of Utpalavati. She once saw a famished woman who had delivered a child and who was on the point of eating her own offspring. Rukmavati was in a dilemma. If she ran home to fetch food for the poor creature, the starving wretch would devour the child in the interval. If she took the child home with her, the mother would perish of starvation. She helped the woman by cutting off her own breasts and giving them to her for food! Indra, the chief of the Devas, appeared on the scene, and she was transformed into a man as a reward for her sacrifice! According to the *Divya-avadana*, she first recovered her limbs by the device of the *saty-adhisthana*. Ksemendra continues the story into Rukmavati's next life. She was born as Sattvavara, the son of the chief of a guild. He took pity on the birds of the air, and cut off bits of his flesh to feed the vultures and other carnivorous birds in the cremation-ground. His eyes were also torn out by the birds, and nothing at last remained of him but a heap of bones.

The famous story of Jimutavahana is related in the *Katha-saritsagara* and the *Avadana-kalpa-lata*, and it is dramatized in Harsa's play, "*Nagananda*". Jimutavahana was a prince, who lived in the forest with his aged father. He was married to a princess, named Malayavati. As he was walking about, he saw on a certain occasion that a boy, named Cankhacuda, was followed by an attendant, who caried two red garments. The boy belonged to the Naga tribe and was chosen as the victim for Garuda, who claimed such a bloody sacrifice every day. His mother was weeping and wailing in the neighbourhood. Jimutarahana offered to give his own life and save the unfortunate creature. In spite of the boy's protests, he donned the red garments and sat on the stone of sacrifice. Garuda came, seized him, and began to devour him. Jimutavahana looked happy and contented. Garuda was astonished at this spectacle, and soon learned his mistake. He expiated his error by repenting for his cruelty, promising to kill no living beings in future, and restoring all the dead Nagas to life.[29] In Harsa's play, the goddess Gauri also appears on the scene and Jimutavahana is restored to life.

Other heroes and heroines of this type are also mentioned in Buddhist literature. Jnanavati, daughter of King Jnanabala, gave her flesh and blood in order to provide medicine for a sick monk.[30] King Punyabala sacrificed his eyes and limbs during many lives. King Surupa gave his body, his queen and his son to be eaten up by a Yaksa, whose form Indra had assumed in order to test the King. King Sarvandada gave refuge to a bird, which was pursued by a fowler. He offered to compensate the poor man by giving him an equivalent weight of his own flesh. But the bird became so heavy in the balance that the king had to sacrifice his whole body in order to keep his promise. He regained it by the usual method of *saty-adhisthana*. Padmaka killed himself in order that he might be reborn as a rohita fish, whose flesh was needed as medicine for curing the sick. King Srisena gave away his wife and half of his own body. Manichuda fed a demon with his flesh and blood. King Maitribala converted some ogres to the true faith by giving them his flesh to eat. In this way the Bodhisattvas dedicated their lives to freed the people from their sufferings.[31]

References:

1. L.B.Horner(tr) *The Book of the Discipline* (Vinaya-Pitaka) Vol.5 *Cullavagga* ix.1.4.
2. Walpola Rahula, *What the Buddha Taught*, Taiwan, 1978, pp16-17.
3. *Visuddhimagga*, P.T.S.P.499.
4. *Samyutta Nikava* V,p.259 *Visuddhimagga*, xvi,35.
5. Rhys Davids; *Buddhist Psychology,* pp.83-86.
6. Walpola Rahula; "Dukkhasatya", *Gauthama ,25th Centinary volume,* edited by N.N.Lew, Delhi, 1956,p.141.
7. Christmas Humphrey; "*Buddhism*" Penguin Books, 3rd edition, 1972, p.81.
8. Stcherbatsky.Th; *The Central Conception of Buddhism*, p.40.
9. Piyadassi Thera; *Buddha's Ancient Path.*
10. Narada; *The Buddha and his teachings*,Malasia, 1988.p.570.
11. De La Valle Poussin; "The Bodhisattva Doctrine" *Encyclopedia of Religion and Ethics,* vol-2,pp.739-53.
12. D.T.Suzuki; *Outlines of Mahayana Buddhism*, London, 1907.p.277.
13. L.D.Barnet; *Encylopedia of Religion and Ethics,* vol.5,p.450.
14. Sir Charles Elict; *Hinduism and Buddhism,* vol.2,p.7.
15. Robert A.F Thurman (tr); *The Holy Teaching of Vimalakirti*, London, 1976,pp. 234,235.
16. Narada, *Op.cit*,p.572.
17. Upali Salgado(ed); *Vesaklipi*-A Buddhist Digest, A Minuwangoda potgul Vihara publication, vol.19, Colombo 2003.
18. Albert Schweitzer; *Indian Thought and its Development* (tr)by Mrs.C.E.B. Russel London, 1951 reprint.
19. *Bodhicharyavatara*,3,6.
20. Sangharaksita(Ed); *Eternal Legacy*, London 1985,p.151.

21. Paul Williams; *Studies in the Philosophy* of *Bodhicharyavatara,* pp.104-114 (Bodhicharyavatara,8:101-3).

22. *Ibid.,* p.153.

23. Geshe Kelsang Gyatso; *Bodhisattva vow*, New Age Books, Delhi 2002,pp.82-83.

24. *Ibid.,* p.86.

25. J.S.Speyer(tr); *The Jatakamala* or Garland of Birth Stories of Aryasura, Motilal Banarsidas, Delhi, 1982,pp.2-8.

26. *Ibid.*, pp.9-19

27. *Avadana Sataka*, vol.I,p.182.

28. Tirumala Ramachandra(tr), *Ksemendruni Avadana Kalpalatha*, Ananda Buddhavihara Trust (Secunderabad 2000).

29. *Ibid.*

30. Haradayal; *The Bodhisattva doctrine in Buddhist Sanskrit Literature*, Motilal Bamarsodas, Delhi, 1978,pp.182-83.

31. Tirumala Ramachandra, *Op. cit*, pp.232-233.

32. *Ibid.*, pp.115-116.

33. *Ibid.*, pp.220-226.

34. *Ibid.*, pp.286-296.

35. *Ibid.*, pp.5-10.

36. *Ibid.*, pp.12-21.

37. *Ibid.*, pp.84-85.

Concept of Dukkha in Buddhist and Jain Traditions

11

Bhagchandra Jain

The concept of Dukkha is the most common feature of both the Śrāmaṇic traditions, Buddhism and Jainism. It is the philosophical central point wherefrom the living being moves in all directions of thoughts and actions. Both the traditions create awareness of death, which is definite, but the time is unsure. Self-realization is there taught through realizing the true nature of things. Life is full of sorrows and sufferings. The real happiness could be achieved by self-efforts based on equality and equanimity.

The Buddha set aside at the outset to reply to the complicated religious questions and kept them as Avyākṛita stating that such vexatious problems are not to be solved by simple arguments. The practical outlook would be more fruitful in removing sufferings.[1] He then preached the four Noble Truths (*Caturāryasatya*), viz. suffering (Dukkha), the origin of suffering (Dukkha-samudya), the extinction of suffering (Dukkha-nirodha), and the path that leads to the extinction of suffering-Aṭṭhāñgikamagga). Avidya (ignorance) is the main cause of suffering which is explained by the introduction of the concept of Pratītyasamutpāda.[2]

Tīrthaṅkara Mahāvīra and his predecessors, on the other hand, replied to such debatable questions through the concept of *Syādvāda* and *Anekāntavāda*. According to Jainism, the suffering of birth and death is called *Sansaraṇa*, and the cause of suffering is *Avidyā* or Mithyātva, which could be destroyed by observing the concept of *Ratnatraya* (Right vision, Right knowledge, and Right conduct).

The object of the present paper is to point out the similarities and dissimilarities on this common point with its comparative approach. We shall discuss here the concept of Dukkha and Avidya in both the traditions.

Concept of Dukkha in Buddhism

The Buddha preached his tenets through two types of Satyas, *Paramārtha* and *Samvṛtti*, which are not of course clearly mentioned in the *Mūla Buddhadeśanā*. But it can be implacable in the concept of suffering. The first group of cause and effect (*Kāryakāraṇa*) tradition starts with Avidyā and culminates to the climax of sufferings while the other one departs from *Samyagdṛṣti* and reaches to the highest point of spiritual development, the *Nirvāṇa*. The first is called *Sāñkleśikadharma* while the other one is named as *Vaivadānika* dharma.

The word Dhamma connotes several meanings in both the traditions in different contexts. I need not go into detail about these connotations. But the opinion of Candrakīrti is worth mentioning where he describes its three connotations, viz. 1) *Tattva* or *Padārtha* (element),2) *Kalyaṇakāraka* (auspicious and propitious), and 3) *Paramārtha* (subtle truth) 2. All the Southern, Eastern and Northern Buddhist sects accept these connotations and describe and investigate the nature of entity on their own accord.

The Jain tradition also favours this exposition of Dharma right from the āgamic to the philosophical period.[3] Two types of Satyas are also introduced in Jainism but they have somewhat different connotations.[4]

The preaching of the Four Noble Truths (*Caturāryasatyas*) is the fundamental tenet of Buddhist philosophy. It commences with the vision of Dukkha (Suffering) and seeks its complete cessation through the observation of *Prajñā*, *Śila* and *Samādhi*. Its voluminous description is found in Pāli and Sanskrit literature[5]. Maharśi Vyāsa, the commentator on the *Pātañjala Yoga*-[6] and Vijñānabhiksu in the *Sāñkhyapravacanabhāṣya*[7] have referred to the Mokṣaśāstra as *Caturvyūhātmaka*, viz. *Roga*, *Rogahetu*, *Roganirodha*- *Ārogya*, and *Bhaisajya* in the medical field. This is the style adopted by the Buddha in preaching the *Caturāyasatyas or Saddharma*. The *Abhidharmakośa Vyākhyā* compares the Buddha in the *Vyādhisūtra* with that of Bhiṣak or physician and *Āryasatyas* with his four parts or divisions.

The existence of Dukkha or adversities cannot be denied at any cost. Some of the Dukkha can be removed through apparent devices but Dukkhas like Jāti (birth), Jarā (old age), Maraṇa (death) etc., are indispensable. This is called Samsāra. The word "Du "(bad) in Dukkha is met with in the sense of vile (Kucchita) and the word "Kham " ("-ness) is met with in the sense of empty (Tuccha). The first Truth is vile because it is the haunt of many dangers and it is empty because it is devoid of the lastingness, beauty, pleasure, and self-conceived by rash people'. So it is called Dukkha[8]. The truth of suffering is given first place since it is easy to understand because of its grossness and because it is common to all living beings.

The *Visuddhimagga* describes seven kinds of suffering, viz. 1) *Dukkha-dukkha* (intrinsic suffering),2) *Vipariṇāma dukkha* (suffering-in-change), 3) *Sankhāra dukkha* (suffering due to formations, 4) *Paṭicchanna dukkha* (concealed suffering), 5) *Apaṭ icchanna dukkha* (exposed suffering), 6) *Paryaya dukkha* (indirect suffering) and 7) *Nisparyaya dukkha* (direct suffering).[9] Mahāvyutpatti divides the Dukkha in two ways. The first division is of three types — Dukkha-dukkhatā, Sanskāra-dukkhatā, and Vipariṇāma-dukkhatā. The second division is of eight types of Dukkhas, Jāti, Jarā, Maraṇa Bhaya, etc. The Abhidharmasamuccaya creates its two main divisions, viz. Samvṛtisatya dukkha and Paramārthasatya dukkha. Three more types of Dukkha are also mentioned there in the Text.[10] Ācārya Śāntideva enumerates only three types of Dukkha in the Sikṣāsamuccaya, viz. Apāyadukkhatā, Yamalokadukkhatā, and Dāridriyadukkhatā.[11] All these types of Dukkhas indicate that the entire world is suffering from Dukkha-Sarvamidam dukkham. In other words, the concepts Panca Upādāna Skandhā Dukktā (Five are suffering Groups of Existence) is the basic concept employed throughout the whole Tripitaka and the Commentaries and other Buddhist literature. It is really Dukkha:

Jāti pi dukkhā, jarā pi dukkhā, vyādhi pi dukkhā, maraṇam pi dukkhā, sokaparidevadukkhadomanassupāyāsā pi dukkhā, sokaparidevadukkhadomanassupāyāsā pi dukkhā, appiyehi sampiyogo dukkho, piyehi vippayogo dukkho, and yampicchiam Na labhati tampi dukkham. Sankhittena pañcupādānakhndhā dukkhā.

Further it is said that there is no smiling, pleasure, in the world that is eternally burning- KO nu hāso kamanando niccam pajjalite sati.[12] Suffering comes forth with the origin. Origin and destruction go together. Nobody knows the starting point of Sansāra. It is the craving (Tanhā) that leads to ever—fresh and repeated rebirths and sense pleasures.

The Abhidharmakosabhāṣya refers to the long debate over the issue of pleasure and suffering held between Sautrāntikas and Vaibhāṣikas. The Vaibhāṣikas ask the question as to why only suffering is included in the Āryasatya, and not pleasure. Replying to the question, the Sautrāntikas state that pleasure is very little in comparison to suffering (Alpatvāt). Even that little pleasure is only a glimpse due to desire, and not the real one. Ācārya Vasubandhu supports his view by citing references from the Buddhist Sūtras.[13] Further in the sixth Kosasthan of the Abhidharmakosa also the Vaibhāsikas strive to establish the existence of pleasure by citing the following verse:

Sanskāranityatām jñātvā atho vipariṇāmatām

Vedanā dukkhatah prokta sambuddhena prajanatā.[14]

The Vaibhāṣikas are of the view that the statement like "Yadkiñcidveditamidamatra dukkhasya" indicates its *Nītārthatā*.[15] All the three types of feeling are there-Sukha, Dukkha, Asukhadukkha.[16] In spite of this, they are not hesitating in accepting the impermanence and unsteadiness of pleasure (Sukha) and express their favourable attitude to the concept of Tridukkhatā.[16]

The sūnyavādi philosopher Nāgārjana composed his Texts माध्यमिक कारिका and रत्नावली with the sole purpose to eradicate the sufferings of beings (प्रयञ्चोपशमार्थम्). Āryadeva followed the same idealogy in the चतुश्शतकम्. He begins the Text showing the method for rejecting belief in permanence which is the main cause of suffering. He says:"One is born in order to die: one is dependent and liable to rebirth. It appears that death is obligatory and life is not.Illness can be cured: old age can be treated. Consequently, you may not fear it, because there is no cure for the final purishment. Clearly you must fear more. It is because of ignorance (मोह) that you did not notice your son's general appearance. Groweing older indicates precisely that he is going to die (1.2.14). Aryadeva uses the ordinary person's fear of death as a motive for the accomplishment of meritorious acts. He advocates मरणानुस्मृति as an antidote for the first erroneous comception."

In the second chapter he advises that one should take care of the body, since merit be accumulated in the course of a long life. He uses the human body as an example of something which ordinary people imagine to be a source of pleasure but which in fact is a source of Dukkha. The third chapter is dedicated to the way of cessation of Dukkha which comes about through understanding its cause, the craving (तृष्णा) for sensual pleasures. He then traditionally criticizes the women's attraction which ensnares others in the cycle of birth and death and condemns all attachment to women. (V.3.1-17).

Āryadeva attacks in chapter four the last of these erroneous conceptions, namely, belief in a real and substantial self. He addresses his remarks on egotism to an unnamed Indian King and advises him that his welfare depends upon the compassionate treatment of the people he protects. In the following chapters he discusses how to eliminate the alflictions (क्लेश) of desire, hatred and confusion (मोह) which arise from attachment to deceptively attractive sense objects. Because both the afflictions and karma work logether to perpetuate bondage in this painfal cycle of birth and death.

Both the Śrāmaṇic religious philosophers stressed since inception on the elimination of suffering in various ways. Entire literature, culture, philosophy, art and architecture are developed on this very point. In fact, Mahākaruṇā in Mahāyāna Buddhism,[17] according to the Āryadharmasaṅgitisūtra, is replaced by the concept of Dukkha; Mahākaruṇā is the main characteristic of the Bodhisattva.[18] who is always ready to bear the adversities of others.[19]

Concept of Dukkha in Jainism

The concept of Dukkha in Jainism is also a central point. Though it is not named as Āryasatya, it has not lesser importance. It can be even divided into four parts like Caturāyasatyas. Dukkha is affliction or ailment (*Pīdalākṣaṇaḥ parināmo duhkham*)[20]. The world is full of sorrows. Birth is painful, old age is painful, and disease and eath are painful. Painful, indeed, is worldly existence, where living beings suffer afflictions.[21]

Dukkha is of four types, viz.1) Svābhāvika or Natural like hot, cold, etc., 2) Naimittika or causal or created by diseases, etc., 3) Sārīrika or corporeal, and 4) Mānasika or mental.[22]. Jain literature describes in detail the various types of sorrows or sufferings that have to be borne by an individual in all the four Gatis, viz. Narakagati, Manuṣyagati, Tiryancagati and Devagati. It is said that sensuous eniovments give momentary pleasure, but prolonged misery, more of misery and less of pleasure and they are the obstructions to salvation and a veritable mine of misfortunes.[23]

Dukkha is the result of Karmas committed. Just as a person is free while climbing a tree but once he starts falling then he has no power to check it. Similarly a living being is free in accumulating the karmas but once accumulated it is beyond his power to control their fruition. Jainism, unlike Buddhism, does believe in the existence of soul. According to it, the pure soul is free from complexes, attachment, blemishes, desire, anger, lust and all other kinds of defects.[24]

Dukkha can be removed by observing the right asceticism. Faith, knowledge and conduct together constitute the path of liberation; this is the path to be followed. The saints have said that if it is followed in the right way it will lead to liberation and otherwise it will lead to bondage.[25]

It can be observed here that there is no difference between Buddhist and Jain attitude towards Dukkha. Both the religions start from the same point and culminate their journey in Nirvāṇa where all the sufferings end. The difference is that the concept of Mahākaruṇā is more developed in Mahāyāna Buddhism.

Concept of Avidyā in Buddhism

The concept of Avidyā (ignorance) in Buddhism commences from the concept of Pratītyasamutpāda (dependent origination), which is considered the main root of Sansarana (birth and death process). Tṛṣna (craving) is its mother and Avidvā is its father.Avidyā covers the capacity of intuiting truth and mistakes in understanding the real nature of Dharma. Sanskāra, Vasanā, Nāma-rūpa, etc., follow the Avivya or Moha (delusion).[26] Nāgārjuna says, "it is due to thinking the things which have no independent nature as eternal, possessed of self, and pleasant that this ocean of existence (Bhava) appears to one who is enveloped by the darkness of attachment and delusion (Moha).[27] If one knows perfectly the nature of Dharma, Tṛṣṇā (carving) naturally ceases. The Vedanā, Vijñāna, Sanjñā, Sanskāra, Nāma-rūpa and other factors close automatically their function and finally the process of birth and death ceases.

In later period, the meaning of Avidyā in Buddhist thought was changed. For instance, the Vijñānavādīs made a distinction between the *Samvrtisatya* (empirical truth) and *Paramārthasatya* (transcendental truth). They termed the avidyā as Moha (delusion) and Viparyāsa (perversion), which cover the real nature of truth. In their opinion, the reality is Parikalpita (imagined), Pāratantra (dependent), and Parinispanna (real or true). An elephant is not real but is an imaginary object by dint of Avidyā.[28] The Sūnyavādīs made it Sūnya, i.e. devoid of any intrinsic reality, yet we know it as a particular object (Parikalpita). The Vijnānavādins denounce the duality of the perceiver and the perceived as false. The creation of the external world is due to the influence of Vāsanā, which is without beginning. The objective world is like an elephant called up by illusion (Māyā-hastin). The creation of an object is imaginary. It may be called Abhūta-parikalpita (unreal imagination). All afflictions (Saṅkleśas) originate from it.[29] It is void (Sūnya) of the perceived and perceiver (Grāhya-grāhaka) even as a rope is the void of snakeness.[30] Maitreyanatha says that the Abhūtaparipalpita cannot be absolutely non-existent because emancipation is held to be due to the destruction of it. The postulation of imagination (Bhrānti), therefore, is necessary for the establishment of emancipation.[31] This is a long discussion held over the subject. Lankāvatāra says: "There is neither Saṅklesa (impurity) nor Suddhi (purification), because there is non-existence of all things (Dharmas). There is neither emancipation nor bondage.[32]

Asvaghośa may also be mentioned in this respect. Regarding the nature, function and annihilation of Avidyā he holds that two aspects may be distinguished in the soul, i.e. the aspect of that ness (Bhūtatathata) and the aspect as the cycle of birth and death (Samsāra). The soul as Bhūtatathatā means the oneness of the totality of all things. The soul as birth and death (Samsāra) comes forth from the Tathāgatagarbha, the ultimate reality. But the immortal and the mortal coincide with each other. Though they are not identical they are not duality either. Thus when the absolute soul assumes the relative aspect by its self-affirmation it is called the all-conserving mind (Alaya-vijñāna). Asvaghosa further describes the process of mind-purification leading to Nirvana.

Pointing out the difference between the idealism of Laṅkāvatāra and the doctrines of Asvaghosa and Nāgārjuna, Dr. Dasgupta says: "The Laṅkāvatāra admitted a reality only as the make-believe to attract the Tirthakas (heretics) who had the prejudice in favour of an unchangeable self (Atman). But Asvaghoṣa plainly admitted an unspeakable reality as the ultimate truth. Nāgārjuna's Mādhyamika doctrines which eclipsed the profound philosophy of Aśvaghoṣa seem to be more faithful to the traditional Buddhist creed and to the Vijanavāda creed of Buddhism as explained in the Lankavatara."[33]

Concept of Avidyā in Jainism

Avidyā in Jainism is used to denote the *Viparyayātmaka Jñāna* (negative or opposite knowledge)[34]. But the term Mithyātva is generally replaced by Avidyā. Likewise, Mithyādarśana, or Mithyādṛṣṭi, Darsanamoha, Moha, etc., are also used in the same sense. Accordingly, the soul is associated with the Karmas, particularly Darsanamoha or Mithyādarsana which obstruct its various capacities of knowing and vision and keep it on roaming in the world. Due to Jñānāvaraṇa and Darśanāvaraṇa, the soul fails to decide the true nature of truth and reality and involves in wrong notion.[35]

Mithyādarśana is divided into many ways. Ācārya Kundakunda divides it into three kinds. viz. Mithyātva (perversity), Ajñāna (nescience), and Avirati (intense attachment)[36]. Unāsvāti divides it into two kinds, Abhigrhīta (Firmly held) and Anabhigrhītta (lightly held).[37] Sivārya refers to the five kinds of Mithyātva viz. Ekānta, Vinaya, Viparīta, Samsaya, and Ajnāna.[38] Pūjyapāda Devanandī keeps it twofold, Naisargika (inborn), and Paropadesapūrvaka (acquired from instructions of others).[39] Akalaṅka refers its 363 types.[40]

Mithvātva is the most powerful Karma, which generates the evils and miseries in one's life. Due to its existence, the soul gets attachment with perverse conduct (Mithyācaritra). On the contrary, Samyagdarśana is a sort of Sraddhāna for the truth, which is discursive determination.[41]. A detailed discussion is available in this regard in Jain philosophical literature.

Samyagdarsana and *Samyagjñāna* are born simultaneously. But they are not identical. They are related as cause and effect, like a lamp and its light. Samyagdarsana is superior to Samyagjñāna inasamuch as the latter derives its appellation "Samyak" from the former. Samyagdarśana can be considered the purified state of consciousness, which enables one to know the truth as it is. It is the ground of Samyagjñāna. Then comes Samyak-cāritra (Right conduct). The combined form of these three prepares the path that leads to the complete emancipation from Karmas (Mokṣa).

Mithyātva or Avidyā is related to Karmic bondage. It is of four types, viz. I) Prkritibandha (configuration or species, ii) Sthiti (duration), iii) Anubhāga (fruitional intensity) and IV) Pradesabandha (karmic mass point or point bondage. The vibration (Yoga) leads to Prkritibandha and Pradesabandha while Kasāyas or passions causes the Sthiti and Anubhāgabandha. Yoga and Kasāya attract the Karmic matter and transform it into karmic body. Yoga is the action of the mind, speech and body due to desire, aversion and cognition. The soul, which is devoid of Yoga and kaṣāyas, has no other reason for bondage of Karmas. It means the Mithyātva is useless (Akincitkara) if it is not with the Yoga and Kaṣāyas.[42]

Jain literature submits the nature of Avidyā or Mithyātva more profoundly.

This is a glimpse of the nature of Dukkha and Avidyā as envisaged by Buddhist and Jain thinkers. The critical and comparative study of the nature of karmas in Buddhism and Jainism could be further made successfully.

References

1. Natthi tam Poṭṭhapādaatthasahitam, na dhammasahitam, na ādibrahmacariyakam, na nibbidāya, na virāgāya, na nirodhāya, na upasamāya, na abhinnāya, na sambodhaya, na nibbānāya samvattati. Tasmātam mayā avyākatam. Dighanikāya, 1.P.15.
2. Mahāvagga, 1,p.3.
3. *Concept of Dhamma in Jainism and Buddhism* by Dr. Bhagchandra Jain published in Dr. A.C.Benarji Felicitation Volume.
4. Samayasāran Ākṁahyati Gathā,14; Pravacanasāra, Tātparyavrtti, 324.
5. Pāli-Dīghanikāya, 2.305-14,p.227; M.Ni.3.249-52, p.334-338; Visuddhimagga, 16.13-104,p.345-361.

   Sanskrit—Lalitavistara, p.303; Abhidharmakosabhāṣya, 6,p.327-33etc.
6. Yalta Cikitsasastram caturvyūham-rogo, rogaheturārogyam bhaiṣajyamiti. Evamidamapi sastrani caturvyūham. Tadyathā samsāraḥ samsāraheturmoksọ moksopāyah. Yogadarsana Bhāṣya, 2.15.
7. Ṣāṅkhyapravacana Bhasya, Adhyayā 1.
8. Visuddhimagga, 16.16.
9. *Ibid.*, 16.35
10. *Ibid.*
11. Sikṣāsamuccaya, p.119.
12. Dhammapada Gāthā, 146.
13. Abhidharmakośa, p.880-882.
14. Abhidharmakośa Bhāsya, p.331.
15. *Ibid.* p.881-882.
16. *Ibid.*6.3p.333.
17. Karunam ca puraskrtya yateta śhubhavṛddhyaye, Sikṣāsamuccaya, Kā.24.
18. *Ibid.* p.151.
19. *Ibid.* p. 148.
20. Sarvārthasiddhi, 6.11 etc.
21. Samaṇasuttam, 55.

22. Nayacakra, 93.
23. Samaṇasuttam, 46.
24. *Ibid.*, 147.
25. *Ibid.*, 193.
26. Visuddhimagga, xvii.
27. Mahāyānavimsikā, verse, 21.
28. Lankāvatārasūtra, x, 374.
29. Esau sarvah sankleso' bhutaparipalpat, Madhyānta, Madhyānta-vibhaṅgasūtra Bhāṣya, p.37.
30. *Ibid.*,p.37.
31. Madhyānta-vibhangasūtra bhāsya-Tīkā,p.18.
32. Lankāvatārāsūtra, x.137
33. *Ibid.*,x.137.
34. Tattvārthavārṭika, 1.1.46; Siddhiviniścaya Tīka, p.747.
35. Samayasāra, Tat. Vr.88,144.
36. Samayasara, 96.
37. Tattvārtabhāsya, 8.1.
38. Bhagawati Ārāshanā, 48.
39. Sarvārthasiddhi.8.1.
40. Rājavārtika, 8.1.
41. Tattvrthasūta, 1.2 with Bhāṣya.
42. Dhavalā, pu.12, 291,1.

Aspects of the Buddhist Social Philosophy-I: Understanding Pañcaśīla

12

Dilip Kumar Mohanta

Tripitaka, the three-fold compilation of the teachings of the Buddha is believed to be the basic literature of Buddhism. The teachings of the Buddha regarding *Dhamma* (doctrine), *Vinaya* (discipline) and *Abhidhamma* (philosophic discourses) are contained in three compilations respectively. As we know, there are three mudrā, distinguishing features of the teachings of the Buddha and they are *Duhkha* (suffering), *Anāttā* (no-soul) and *Anicca* (impermanence). The doctrinal and discipline level teachings are interconnected, and any fruitful discussion of one presupposes the other. The fundamental teachings of the Buddha have been subsumed under four noble truths, namely, the truth of Suffering, the truth of the origin of Suffering, the truth of Cessation of Suffering, and the truth of the Way leading to the Cessation of Suffering (*Duḥkha, Duḥkha-samudaya, Duḥkha-nirodha and Duḥkha-nirodha-gāmini pratipat*). Any discussion on ethical matters would thus become meaningful only if it is considered in the light of the doctrinal aspect beginning with suffering. Ethical behaviour (*śila*), concentration (*samādhi*) and wisdom (*prajñā*) constitute the foremost moral duties for individuals living in society. Considered from the sociological point of view the number and strictness have been modified and emphasized in the moral code of conduct. But the the basic goal remains the same, that is, to eradicate suffering. Therefore a short analysis of suffering (*Duḥkha*) will precede our discussion on ethical matters.

Duḥkha: The spectrum of the word '*duḥkha*' is wide. The philosophical implication of this word is both factual and ethical. Everything is suffering:

"*Birth is suffering, so is old-age, disease and death*...union with what we like is suffering, so is separation from what we like or love and so is the desired unfulfilled. In short, five aggregates for 'grasping' (five sets constituting our psycho-physical existence) is suffering"[2] (trans. Matilal, 2002, p.282).

Suffering is the most vivid fact of life. It has three varieties. The ordinary variety of it is known as *dukkha-dukkha*. It includes all forms of suffering both physical and mental. The above-quoted passage mainly depicts this type of suffering. The second form of suffering is called *saṇkhāra-dukkha*. It is to be understood in the context of our state of being as conditionally originated. So it is known as the suffering of conditioned states. The import of this form of suffering is related to one's very- 'being-in-the world' (Heidegger). It refers to the universal law of conditionality. Even the feeling of happiness is *dukkha,* because everything being conditionally arisen, dependently existent is impermanent and the pleasure-feeling is accompanied by the fear of impermanance and so it is also suffering in the ultimate analysis. The third form of suffering is *Vipariṇāma dukkha*. As already said in the preceding form of suffering that the so-called happy or pleasant situation changes or disappears due to the principle of change. Whatever is apparently pleasant, desirable, is subject to change and ultimately suffering becomes unavoidable. Thus goes the verse of *Dhammapada,* 277:

"All created things are sorrowful, when one by wisdom realizes (this) he heeds not (is superior to) this world of sorrow, this is the path of purity." (Eng. tr. S. Radhakrishnan, 1950).[3]

The purpose of the disciplines in Buddhism is to prepare oneself for the eradication of all forms of suffering. Suffering is conditionally arisen and therefore any hope for its cessation means the cessation of its conditions. And from this teleological and evaluative concern, the Buddha taught the eightfold path for the cessation of suffering. Suffering is thus to be understood not only as a descriptive fact of our existence but also as an 'evaluative' expression in the teachings of the Lord Buddha. As an integral philosophy of life, the Buddha's teaching contains the physical, mental and soteriological aspects of our existence. It is interesting therefore to see in contrast to the eight steps of noble path, there are the eight types of sin arising out of different *misdeeds*. In his prescriptive sermons the Buddha followed the *middle path avoiding the exclusive self-indulgence and exclusive self-mortification.* This is reflected in his treatment of *śīla, samādhi* and *prajñā* as gradual steps towards *nirvāna* (in *pāli nibbāna*).[4] The moral code of conduct is supposed to purify our outward behaviour and by disciplining one's behaviour or physical conduct one can become a true member of a prosperous society. Social life is ultimately dependent upon the life-pattern of its individual members. So in character-building the foremost importance is given by the Buddha to *Śīla-māhātmya*. Side by side of the physical discipline, the Buddha prescribed mental disciplines for the purification of mind through concentration (*samādhi*). *Prajñā* or wisdom is the realization that everything-physical or mental whatever, is suffering (*dukkha*), impermanent (*anicca*), non-substantial (*anātta*) and therefore there would be no *'craving for'* and *clinging to'* and as a result no 'becoming' (*bhava*) any more. However, here we shall deal only with '*Śīla*'. Amongst the eightfold path for the cessation of suffering right speech (*Samyak vāk*), right action (*samyak karmānta*) and by suggestively right living (*samyak ājīva*) constitute śīlatattva, the moral principles of conduct in the broad sense. In a narrower sense it means right action and right speech.

II

The sanskrit word śīla (pāli *sīla*) means *sadācāra*-right behaviour and conduct. By *sadācāra* the following of moral disciplines in life is meant.[5] The Lord Buddha prescribed five śīlas for the householders and in some special occasions they are advised to follow three more. So *'pañcaśīla'* and *'astaśīla'* are meant for householders. But for the *śramanas* and *Bikkhus/Bikkhunis,* the minimum number of *śīla* to oblige are ten (*daśa*) and it has been increased later up to two hundred twenty seven corresponding to new complexities that has been arising along with the extension of the monastic way of life.[6] For this type of increase in the number of precepts is a clear indication to the recognition of the importance of public opinion in the changed circumstances.

The word *'śīla'* though means the purification of speech and action in phyical level, it in fact, includes consciousness. In the Buddhist vocabulary *'cetanā'* (consciousness) is sometimes called *karunā* (considering its background role in all human activities). (As the Buddha says, *'cetanā' ham bhikkhave kammam vadāmi. Centayitvā kammam karoti hinam vā paniltam vā*).[7] The *Dīghanikāya, gathā* no 183, prescribes abstinence from doing all kinds of wrong or sin is called *'śīla'*. "The ten cardinal *'sins'* are: 1. Killing, 2. stealing, 3. sexual misconduct, 4. lying, 5. slander, 6. harsh talk, 7. frivolity, 8. covetousness, 9. ill-will and 10. false views."[8] So sila means absentience from committing all these.[9] Though predominantly *'śilas'* are negative precepts in Buddhism, they have by implication positive moral bearings. Let us explain the śīla prescribed under *samyak vāk,* right speech.

There are four types of speech abstinence, namely,1) *Mṛṣāvācavirati*-avoidance of speaking untrue,2) *Piśunavāca-varati*-avoidance of slandering others, by creating discords among people and making one anothers' foe by distorted or doctored speech,3) *Paruṣavāca-virati*-avoidance of harsh speech and4) *Sampralāpa-virati*-avoidance of talkative-ness or unnecessary speech. All these four kinds of restraints to be maintained in speech are considered as moral actions, because they pre-suppose the volitional act of the agent of speech. A person is free to choose any of the two alternatives-to maintain abstinence or not. If a person follows the abstinence, his outward behaviour becomes purified and as a result it will lead towards the cessation of suffering. But if a person does not culture these abstinence, he is exposed to commit sin and as a result he would be revolving through suffering from birth to birth. Though pre-dominantly it is in the form of abstinence and a negative sense it conveys, but as a matter of fact it suggests positive *ought* which is good for the individual as well as for society. So the prescription here includes two more obligations. Its meaning is not limited within the boundary of a particular individual's abstinence from speaking what is untrue, from slandering others and sowing the seeds of discord among others, from speaking harsh words or from speaking meaningless and unnecessary matters. It also includes volitional discouraging of others from speaking unture, from slandering others or making false accusation, from meaningless talking. And lastly it also includes volitional effort on the part of individual in family, in social life not to sanction any of these four types of sinful acts through speech. What is seen here by positive implication is that in society, in family and in one's indivudual life according to Buddhism, it is obligatory to speak the truth, to take active role so that others are encouraged to speak the truth and to sanction only what is true. It advises us to speak sweetly so that other's sentiments are not injured, to encourage others in soft and sweet speaking and in family and societal assemblies to sanction this quality-speech. It is an indication to encourage logicality and deliberation in assembles as well as in families. The *Dhammika-suttas* nos 18-23, of *Suttanipāt* thus explain the spirit of this precept of right speech (*samyak vāk*) and this reveals the social relevance of the first precept taught by the Buddha. A *piśunavāca* person is a sadist and the root of many evils in society. He creates enemity among friends, strengthens friendship among friends. A person with the culture of these four types of conduct and behaviour in speech is an asset in society. So the advice goes under the first precept (*śīla*) is to speak the truth, encourage to speak the truth and to sanction what is true, be sweet speaking, encourage others and sanction this only; to maintain integrity in speech, to encourage integrity in the speech of others and to sanction the speech with integrity; to speak meaningfully and logically, to encourage such speech, and to sanction this type of speech with priority. This includes the encouragement for maintaining mutual trust, co-operation and understanding among individuals, groups, communities and at large among humanity. In today's society which has been suffering because of the lack of minimum sense of honesty and fair play such a moral precept can show some light of hope even in the distant horizon for the survival of humanity. A follower of right speech has been appreciated in different canonical literature[10] as *'samagjārām, samagjarata, samaganāndi* and *samagjakarana'*. He is a tie of love and peace in society.[11] A very important aspect of this *śīla* (-moral precept) is that it makes mandatory for people to refrain form all kinds of deceptive practices even in speech, because it is a source of rising disintegration in society.

The second among the five precepts (*pañca-śīla*) is known as *'samyak karmānta'* - performing right action. It has four types:

a) *Adattādānavirati* the precept of not taking what is not given or due to oneself. It does not sanction any kind of deceptive practices, encouragement of such practices, say bribery, dishonest earning, etc., nor allows any sanction in favour of any such sinful acts. To break this moral ought is the same as stealing which is considered as one of ten cardinal sins. In the positive aspect, it suggests the paying of respect for others' right and possession. It helps the society to maintain integration and reduces inequality among its members. The practice of this precept helps to keep the society free from corruption at large. Abstention from excessive possession by dishonest means keeps the society 'corruption-free' and this in turn helps in its development and progress. It indirectly encourages *dāna*, the practice of donation in society.

b) *Prāṇatipāta-virati*-It is the precept of abstinence from killing, of not encouraging anybody for killing and of not sanctioning anybody's act of killing. It is, in fact, the practice of non-violence. The excessive slaughtering of animals in the name of yajña has been kept in mind in formulating this precept. It does not only mean abstention from murder but also from any kind of injury to others-both physical and non-physical. It is in turn an active attempt in recognizing the value of others' lives and equal respect for the lives of all. In ecological paraphrase, we may say that it is an indirect indication to the fact of our life as inter-dependent and therefore doing any harm to any creature is the same as doing harm to one's own existence. It is also the recognition of life as one. The *Dhammapada*, no 390 thus reads, "the places where the mind is refrained from violence are the places where there cannot be any more suffering (*-yatho yato himsamano nivattati, tato, tato sammatimeva dukkham*).[12] 'There is nothing greater than doing good to all beings' (*Nāsti hi kaṃmataraṃ sarvalokahitapā*)[13]

c) *Kamesumicchācāra-virati-* Abstention from committing 'sexual misdeeds' is another precept under right action. The word *kāma* is used in the locative plural form and the true import of this word here is the abstention from misdeeds related to the use of the five sense organs. If we are free to act, we may choose body, mind and speech to unlawful indulgence. It also restricts any kind of unbridled or uncontrolled freedom for enjoyment and thus makes a householder to practise the middle way avoiding the extremes of unlimited sensual pleasure and the absolute form of mortification. Unrestricted pursuit of sensual enjoyment is the door to invite sufferings to family life on the one hand and to corrupt social order on the other. It is indeed true that in this diseased age, because of moral laxity we suffer a lot. The positive implication of this precept is that it is obligatory to respect other persons' wives as one's mother, sister and daughter. And for a female individual it is obligatory to respect others' male counterparts, as father, brother and son. This culture of moral behaviour will surely create a sense of mutual respect, love and affection in society.

The last and fourth precept under pañcaśīla is the abstention from intoxication (*surāmoureya madya mādakārtha-virati*). It like the previous one includes not to encourage anybody to be intoxicated and not to sanction any kind of intoxication by anybody at any cost in society.[14] This precept has immense sociological significance. From our empirical study of society we know that any kind of intoxication muddles the mind of the individual and it creates an atmosphere of social disharmony. Disharmony in societal level not only disturbs our family but also questions our survival and existence. An intoxicated person is a menance to society, because he begets debauchery, gambling and many other social evils. These four types of right action with right speech having its three varieties are known as *pañcaśīla*, five precepts or the barest minimum as obligatory for any householder in society. *Samyak ājīva* or right livelihood has only a derivative significance because it sanctions only the professions that "do not involve the performing of prohibited actions as means of livelihood"[15] Therefore though it has been included in '*pañcaśīla*', it is not considered a constituent in the primary sense of the precepts.[16]

It is to be noted here that, apart form these five precepts, another group of three, namely, 1) *Vikālabhujana veramani-* abstention from taking untimely meal (or taking meal in the afternoon), 2) *Nācca-gīta vādita-visūka-dassana,* or 3) *mālāganadha-vilepana-dhārana mandana-vibhūsanatthānā vermani-* abstention from enjoying dancing singing, music, witnessing grotesque mime, or refraining from using garlands, perfumes, cosmetics and personal adornments, and 4) *Uccāśayana mahāsayanā veramani-* abstention from taking high seats. This is prescribed, because high seat signifies social prestige and this inflates our ego. These additional three taking either no 3 or 4 are to be observed on *uposatha* days , the special days for fasting and mediation or performing religious ceremonies. In short *pañcaśīla* means 1) truthfulness, sweetness and integrity in speech, 2) not killing or practice of non-violence in thought, speech and action, 3) not stealing, 4) not performing sexual and other sensual misconduct and 5) not to be intoxicated. In *Vinaya-pitaka, Mahāvaggo prakarana* (no. 1.3.12) ten precepts have been prescribed for the Buddhist *śramanas.* In addition to the first five precepts and total four of the second order (i.e. precepts that are to be observed under obligation by a house holder only on the special days of fasting and meditation or religious ceremonies), *jātarūpa-rajat-parigraha-virati-* abstention from accepting gold and silver, that is to say, valuable materials are prohibited for a person who has opted for monastic life. So for a Bhikku who has opted for a monastic life, the practice of 'daśaśīla' becomes obligatory.[17]

With strict adherence to the precepts that are outwardly in the form of what ought not to be done, without the admission of forbidden deeds an individual is encouraged to maintain his means of livelihood. The contraries to the forbidden things are to be understood as morally obligatory. In accordance with this line of demarcation what *ought* not to be done is called *vāritraśīla-* expressed in the form of abstention and what is considered as ought to be done either directly in the teaching of the Buddha or indirectly considered as duty by implication of the various forms of abstention is described as *cāritraśīla*-duty to be performed. Both are complementaries, two sides of the same coin.

III

The *pañcaśīla*, the five precepts prescribed for the householders by the Buddha have a deep social significance. It not only encourages an indivudual to earn one's bread but also encourages one to keep vigilance upon oneself so that one could maintain one's livelihood without causing any harm and exploitation to others. In the present day world, if these could be extended to the political personalities of national or international sphere, at least our existence would not have been threatened, there would not have been a cold war or star war,- there would not have been death from starvation and the like.[19] The Buddha's ideal stands for the seeking of the individual's good in and through the promotion of collective good. To illustrate the practice of benevolence (*maitri*) to all creation and compassion (*karuṇā*) to the distressed the Buddha refers to the story of a mother who tries to protect her only child even at the cost of her own life. So the Master's advice is to follow the abstention from misdeeds and the performing of the moral ideal of loving-caring behaviour to all living creatures. This is the way of moral purification and the way of character building for the good of all. Ultimately it is the character, the intergrity and the wisdom of those who live in the society that would determine its fate. We should strive towards a social environment where honesty and integrity are virtues that really pay. *"Savve satta bhavantu sukhitattā."*

References

1. The word *pitaka* in Pāli literally means a basket. Since each compilation of the Buddha's teachings were carried in a separate basket in the first Council in 483 B.C. and the compiled subject-matters were classified into three heads, these are known by the blanket term *tripitaka*. The *Vinaya pitaka* contains the disciplines of the Buddhist way of life. The *Sutta-pitaka* is the collection of the utterances of the Master himself (*buddha vacana*) and its five constituent parts are usually known as nikāyas (i.e. *Dīgha, Majjhima. Anguttara, Samyutta* and *Khuddaka*). Being requested by *Mahākaśyap*, Ānanda recited the dialogues on the doctrine (*Dharma*) and Upali recited the disciplines (*Vinaya*), and as a result *Suttapitaka* and *Vinaya pitaka* were compiled. The third compilation contains philosophical investigations and is known as *Abhidharma pitaka*. This is believed to be 'derivative of the recital of Ananda, (Matilal, 2002, p. 281). In the *Suttapitaka* the word *dharma* has been used as doctrines. But in *Abhidharma pitaka*, the word *dharma* is taken to mean elements of reality and the compound word *abhidharma* thus means philosophical

investigations about the elements of reality. Apart from *tripitaka, Visuddhimagga, Mahavamsa, Dīpavamsa, Milindo-panho* are also important sources of understanding early Buddhism.

2. The Pali text *Vibhaṇga* contains this passage. One may see Bhikkhu Jagadis Kassapa's *saccavibhaṇga* p. 126. One may also see *Vibhaṇga* (ed. by) Rhys Davids, C.A.F., Pali Text Society, 1934. However the Pali text goes as:

   Jāti pi dukkhā, jarā pi dukkhā, maraṇaṃ pi dukkhām, sokaparideva-dukkha domanassupāyāsā pi dukkhā appiyehi sampayogo dukkho, piyehi vippāyogo dukkho yaṃ picchaṃ na labhati taṃ pi dukkhaṃ saṃkhittena Pañcupādanakkhandhā dukkhā.

3. *Dhammapada, gāthā no,* 277.

   Sabbe saṇkhārā dukkhā, ti yadā paññāya passati/
   Antha nibbinadati dukkhe, esa maggo visuddhiyā.//

4. *Nirvāṇa* etymologically means 'to blow out'. It stands for extinction of taṇhā, craving for what is thought to be pleasant and clinging to it. *Tuṇhā* is interpreted sometimes as *vaṇā* in the sense that it weaves a link between one life with another. The following of the eightfold path strictly according to Bhuddhism leads to the extinction of suffering, the cessation of *saṃsāra.*

5. Both in the *Mahābhārata* and the *Manusamhita* the word *sadācāra* signifies morality and a moral person is described as *'śīlavān'.*

6. *Goutam Buddhera Dharma O Darśana* (in Bengali) by Sukomal Chudhury, Mahabodhi Agency, Kolkata, 1997, p. 53.

7. *Ibid.*, p. 55.

8. B.K. Matilal, in *Philosophy, Culture & Religion* series, see, *Mind Language* and *World*, (ed.) J. Ganeri, Oxford University Press, 2002, p. 284.

9. *"Savva papassa akaraṇaṃ kusalassa upasampadā saci'a pariyodapanam atam buddhānusāsanam."*

10. See, *Majjhima-Nikāya,* Culahatathipadopamasutta, no. 27, *Mahātaṇhāsamkhayasutta, no.* 38, *sāleyyasutta, no.* 41.

11. See, also *The Dīgha-Nikāya,* Śrāmaṇya-phala-sutta (Bengali trans. by Bhiksu Śīlabhadra, Mahabodhi Book Agency, Kolkata 1997 edition, Part-I, nos. 43-63, pp. 53-59.

12. *Dhammapada*, (Bengali trans. by Bhikkhu Śīabhadra, 3rd ed.) Maha Bodhi Book Agency, Kolkata, 1999, p. 104.

13. *Stone Inscriptions* of Aśoka, the 6th inscription. The Bible also asks people to be compassionate and to abstain from violence. Proverbs 10.12 reads as "Hatred stirreth up strifes, but love covereth all sins". ......Romans: XII.20 reads also, "If thine enemy hunger, feed him, if he thirst give him drink." Dhammapada's conjugal verse no 5 contains this universal message of love and discourages people from fighting as foes.

    Na hi verena verāni sammantīdha kudācanam/
    Aberena ca sammanti, asa dhamma sanatano//

14. See, *Sutta-nipāt*, pp. 393-398; also see *Dhammika-sutta* pp. 18-23, (ed. by Dines Anderson and Helmer Smith) London, Pali Text Soceity, 1965; also see/ *Suttanipata Commentary*, Vols-III, by the same editors, originally published 1916-1918, reprint, 1977-1989.

15. P.T. Raju: *Structural Depths of Indian Thought*, South Asian Publishers, New Delhi, 1985, p. 151.

16. The *pancaśīla*, moral disciplines for purification of individual's physical behaviour and conduct has an overtone to pursue a balanced and proper means of livelihood. Accordingly, the Buddhist canonical literatures encourage a lay follower to abstain from the profession of dealing in arms, poison, flesh, living beings and intoxicants.

17. *Buddhagosa's Visuddhimagga,* (part I, Para 25-142) discusses different kinds of śila in detail. 2 vols. Ed. by Rhys Davids, London, Pali Text Society, 1920, 1921 and reprint as one volume 1975.

18. *Mātā yathā niyam puttaṃ āyusā akaputtam anurakkhe/*
    Avaṃ pi savvabhūtesu mānasaṃ bhāvaye aparinamāṇam//

    For details see. S. Chodhury's *Goutama Buddhere Dharma O Darsana* (in Bengali), Mahabodhi Book Agency, Kolkata, 1997, p. 55-56.

19. It may be noted in passing that Mahatma Gandhi's caution to modern human beings is interesting. Action or performing anything without honesty, integrity and with selfish motive is considered by Gandhi as *sin*. He listed seven of such sins. These are: (1) Politics without principles, (2) Wealth without work, (3) Pleasures without conscience, (4) Knowledge without character, (5) Commerce without morality, (6) Science without humanity and (7) Worship without sacrifice.

Concept of Suffering in Early Buddhism

13

Bimalendra Kumar

The truth which was realized by Lord Buddha under the Bodhi tree is called as Noble Truths (*Arya Satya*). These four truths may be considered as the root cause of the Buddha's order. The knowledge of these four noble truths was realized by the Buddha at the time of his getting enlightenment. He had preached this in his first sermon at Ṛṣipatana Mṛgadāva[1]. Due to enlightenment of these four truths, the Lord is called the Buddha[2]. The knowledge of the *dhamma* means to know the four noble truths[3]. Again what the Buddha attained in enlightenment is *Dhamma* and what he preached or hesitated to teach is *Dhamma* — *"Adhigato kho me ayam dhammo"*[4]; *"Kicchenadhigato dhammo halam dani pakāsitum"*[5]; *"Desito* ,mayā dammo *anantaram abāhiram Katvā"*[6]. *Dhamma* is what is proclaimed, taught, instructed — *akkhāto desanā, sāsana, anusāsana,* but it is in its essence not an intellectual doctrine to be logically comprehended, *attakkāvacaro*. The *dhamma* has to be adopted as a way of life, to be practised. It is a path to be trodden (*maggo, patipadā*) so that it may lead to immediate personal realization[7].

Thus, *Dhamma* is psycho-ethical thought and practice which takes its being from the state of suffering to the state of eternal bliss. It is just like a raft (*Kullupama*) going from this shore to the other of the river full of stormy waves[8]. The Buddha declared that after him the *dhamma* would be the teacher in his place. In this way *dhamma* spans a variety of meanings, namely, teaching[9], law[10], nature[11] composite and non-composite things[12], moral and immoral state[13], action[14], and reality[15].

The equivalent term for Truth in Pali is *Sacca*, which means 'that which is'. The heart of the Buddha's teaching is the Four Noble Truths (*Cattāri Ariya Saccāni*), which he expounded in his very first sermon viz. *Dhammacakkapavattanasutta*. These truths are so called because they were discovered by the Greatest Ariya, the Buddha — "Yasmā panetāni buddhādayo ariyā pativijjhanti, tasmā ariyasaccānīti vuccanti"[16]. Or, these truths were experienced by the Buddha and nobles, therefore, it is called the Noble truths — "Ariyānam saccāni ariyasaccāni". Or, the perfect enlightenment of these truths can be achieved by the nobles, therefore, they are called as Nobles truths — "ariyā imāni pativijjhanti, tasmā ariyasaccāni ti vuccanti"[17]. Lord Buddha himself has told that the Tathagata is noble among the World of God and men and this is the truth of nobles, therefore, this is noble truth — "*Sadevake, bhikkhave, lokesadevamanussāya tathagato ariyo, tasmā ariyasaccāni ti vuccanti"[18]. Again he says that "Imāni, kho, bhikkhave, cattāri ariyasaccāni tathāni, avitathāni, anannathani, tasma ariyasaccāniti vuccanti*". The four noble truths are namely —

1. There is suffering — dukkhaṃ ariyasaccaṃ,
2. There is a cause of suffering — dukkha-samudayaṃ ariyasaccaṃ,
3. There is cessation of suffering — dukkha nirodhaṃ ariyasaccaṃ and,
4. There is a path, which leads towards the cessation of suffering — dukkhanirodha gāmani paṭipadā ariyasaccaṃ.

The four noble truths have been discussed in different suttas specially in *Mahāsatipatthānasutta* of *Dighanikāya*[19]. There it is said- '*Tattha katamaṃ dukkhaṃ ariyasaccaṃ*'. In answer to this, it is said that "birth is suffering, decay is suffering, disease is suffering, death is suffering, to be united with the unpleasant is suffering, to be separated from the pleasant is suffering, not to receive what one desires is suffering, in brief, the five Aggregates of attachment are suffering"[20]. It is clear from the above statements that all things of the world are associated with suffering or the forms of the suffering. They are suffering not only because of originating from the suffering but they are suffering by nature themselves. It is said in the commentary that they are called as suffering because of having four reasons — "dukkhassa pīlanattha, sankhaṭṭho, sanatāpaṭṭho, viparināmaṭṭho ime cattāro dukkhassa dukkhassa dukkhaṭṭha tathā avitathā anannathā"[21]. Again, the etymological derivation of the word dukkha has been done by Acarya Buddhaghosa — "du iti ayam saddo *kucchite dissati, 'kham' saddo pana tucche Ṁ idam ca pathamasaccam kucchitam anekaupaddavadhitthanato, tuccham Ṁ dukkham ti vuccati*"[22]. The feelings which are unloved, opposite to mind, disagreeable, etc. are called suffering[23]. The Blessed one also says that this is the suffering, this real, this is known and not other. It is said that —

> "*Nā bādhakaṃ yato dukkhaṃ, dukkhā annam na bādhakam bādhakattaniyāmena, tato saccaṃ idaṃ mataṃ*"[24].

From the above sources, it is said that the world is full of suffering. Each moment of the life is associated with the suffering. Human beings are annoyed and perplexed by this. This suffering is real, truth and since this has been propounded by the Tathagata, it is called a 'Noble truth'.

In *Vibhanga-prakaraṇa*, each part of the first noble truth-dukkha ariyasacca has been explained. Jati or birth has been explained- the meaning of Jati is to take birth, to appear, to create, to get form of skandhas (aggregates) etc. — *Jātīti ayaṃ jātisaddo anekaattho. Tathā hesaṃ "ekaṃ pi jāti, dve pi jātiyo ti ettha bhave āgato... Yatohaṃ bhaginī, ariyāya jātiyā jāto ti ettha ariyasīle*"[25]. In real, when the uniting consciousness comes out from the womb of the mother and first appearance of the aggregates of a being is called as jati or birth. It is said that — "*khandhā yena hi paramatthato pātubhavanti, na sattā, pātubhāvo ti uppati...ayam vuccati jāti ti ayam jāti nāma kathīyati*"[26]. In other words, it is the arising of a birth consciousness, technically called *patisandhi-citta*. It is the re-arising of any one of the nineteen types of resultant consciousness (two *upekkha sahagata-santīrana ahetuka-vipākas*, eight resultant consciousness of *Kamāvacāra*-moral, technically called *Mahāvipāka*, five resultant consciousness of *Rupāvacāra* moral and four resultant consciousness of *Arūpāvacara*-moral consciousness), which function as *Patisandhi* or uniting one state of existence with another. It takes place in the first moment of entering of the being into the womb of a mother. Thus, birth or jāti is the furtherance of life continuum where there is the integration of the five aggregates or emergence of the twelve bases — "*khandhānam pātubhāvo, āyatanānam paṭilābho*"[27]. It is just like the revolving of the wheel of a chariot from one state to another i.e. death to birth —

> "*Iccevaṃ mattasattānām, punadeva bhavantare,*
> *paṭisandhimupādāya tathārupam, pavattati*"[28].

The term *jara* (decay) is the learning of the being towards the destruction in the flow of impermanence. It may be understood that there are two expressions of it, namely; *khanika-jarā* and *pākatajarā*. The former is the name of momentary decay. Every moment, the being in existence, moves towards it. In the functional nature of reality, there are arising and ceasing in every moment. It starts from the second moment of existence and continues till arising of *cuti-citta*. The latter is the name of apparently visible decay. When the body is broken, it becomes weak and pale,the bones become visible through the thin layers skin, wrinkles apper on the face, hairs become grey, we with a sense of grief say — "old age has come"[29]. Here both the forms of decay are meant as *jarā*. *Jarā* has the characteristic of fruition (*paripāka*) of aggregates, it has the function to take one towards death and it appears with the destruction of youth[30].

Death (*marana*) has several names like — *maccu, mara, yama, antaka, marana*, etc. Its taking place is presented by the expressions like — fall out of a state (*cuti*), the dropping out of it (*cavanata*), the dissolution (*bhedo*), disappearance (*antaradhānam*), the accomplishment of the life term (*kālakiriya*), the breaking of the groups (*khandhānam bhedo*), the laying down of the body (*kalavarassa nikkhepo*) breaking of life vitality (*jīvitindriyassupachelo*), etc.[31] Really speaking, it is purely a psychoethical phenomenon-intrinsically psychological and functionally ethical. In clear terms, it is the arising of a consciousness known as *Cuti-citta* (dying consciousness). The last moment of the present life is the *cuti*. It is an act of cutting down or discontinuing the process of present life. This act is performed by the consciousness which we name *Cuti-citta*. It is any one of the nine types of resultant consciousness, namely — one investigating consciousness, moral resultant and eight great resultants of sensual sphere of consciousness (*kāmāvacara citta*). Each of these nine types of resultant consciousness has the potentiality of appearing as *Cuti-citta*. Arising in this way, it makes the total exhaustion of the mental and material life-force (*nāma jīvitindriya* and *rūpajīvitindriya*) and puts a stop of the generation of material qualities. As a result of that, the body falls flat on the ground just like an unconscious wooden log. We name this state as death (*marana*).

Lord Buddha, while instructing the first noble truth, has taken *soka, parideva, dukkha, domanassa, upāyāsa*, etc., as suffering. *Soka* has been described as a term of mental, unpleasant feeling. It arises with the destruction of birth, things, false views, etc. — '*nātivyasanena* na phutthassa bhogavyasanena phuttahassa dukkhadhammena *phuttahassa soko, socanā socitattam antosoko antoparisoko cetaso parijjhāyatanā domanassam soksallam ... ayam vuccati soko*'[32]. Suffering is the name of a disagreeable feeling of the body — *yam kāyikam asātam kāyikam dukkham kāyasamphassajam asātaṃ dukkham vedayitam kāyasamphassajā asātā dukkhā vedanā — idam vuccati dukkham*[33]. Mental unpleasant feeling or *domanassa* has been defined as the unbearable feeling of psychic factors — '*cetasikam asatam cetasikam dukkham cetosamphassajam asātam dukkham vedayitam cetosamphassaja asātā dukkhā veda*nā'[34]. The suffering, which arises due to the destruction of the birth, is called as lamentation (*upāyāsa*). It has the characteristics of burning the consciousness[35].

Just as philosophically *cetana* and *kamma* are synonymous so also are *kama* and *dukkha* synonymous. The reason is pain: the kamas invariably result in pain —

> *Dukkhā kamā, Eraka, na sukhā kāmā, Eraka /*
> *Yo kāme kāmayati, dukkhaṃ so kāmayati, Eraka //*[36]

Because the *kāmas* always result in pain, the latter becomes another name for the former — *dukkhaṃ ti, bhikkhave, kāmānametam adhivacam*[37].

The Buddha says, "Monks, previously as well as now too, I preach only two things — suffering (dukkha) and its cessation (nirodha)"[38]. For the cessation of the suffering, he prescribed the tristepped eight fold path, which constitutes the Four Noble Truths — *Dukkhanirodhagāmanipatipadā ariyasacca*. In the *Dhammapada*, it is said

Eseva maggo natthanno dassanassa visuddhiyā /
Etaṃ hi tumhe patipannā dukkhassanta karissatha //

The eightfold path (*aṭṭhangiko maggo*) is also known as the 'Middle Path' (*Majjhima patipadā*), because it avoids two extremes. It is to be noted that a mere knowledge of the path, however complete, will not do. In this case, our function is to follow it and develop it — "*dukkhanirodha gāmani-paṭipadā ariyasaccam bhāvetabbam*"[39]. A person, who has a certain amount of confidence in the doctrine, equips himself with the theory of the Four Truths. Having right intention and some understanding he conforms to virtue and practises discrimination of principles. He concentrates his will, thought, energy and investigations and so increases his self-possession and goes on to practise concentration, developing joy in this practice and tranquillity of body and thought, so that his meditations bring him to equanimity. Then his understanding can exercise its full potentiality and he should be able to attain enlightenment, to verify in his own experience, understand in their true nature, the Four Truths.

References

1. *Mahāvagga* (Ed.) Bhikkhu J. Kashyap, Nalanda, 1959, p. 13.
2. "Vujjhitā *Saccānīte Buddho, bodhetā pajāyati Buddho*" — *Mahāniddesa* (Ed.) Bhikkhu J. Kashyap, Nalanda, p. 457. *"Imesam kho, bhikkhave, catunnaṃ ariyasaccanam. Yathābhūtam abhisambuddhattā tathāgato araham. Sammāsambuddho ariyā ti vuccatīti* — *Samyuttanikāya*, Bhikkhu J. Kashyap, Nalanda Edition.
3. *Udāna* (*Khuddakanikāya*, Vol. I), Nalanda Edition, 1959, p. 2.
4. *Majjhimanikāya* (Nalanda Edition), Vol. I, p. 217.
5. *Ibid.*, (*Bodhirājakumārasutta*), Vol. II, p. 318-343.

6. *Dīghanikāya* Vol. II *(Mahāparinibbānasutta)* Ed. Bhikkhu J. Kashyap, Nalanda Edition, p. 58 ff.
7. *Samyuttanikāya* Vol. II. (Ed.). Bhikkhu J. Kashyap, Nalanda Edition, *(Dhammābhisamaya)*, p. 134.
8. *Majjhimanikaya*, Vol. I, *op. cit.* p. 179.
9. *"Deseti dhammam ādikalyānam, majjhekalyānam pariyosānakalyānam .."* *Dighanikāya*, Vol. I, p. 55.
10. *"Esa dhammo sanantano"* — *Khuddakanikāya*, Vol. I, (Ed.) Bhikkhu J. Kashyap, Nalanda Edition, p. 17.
11. *"Chedana-vinddhasana-dhammo"* — *Dīghanikāya*, Vol. I, p. 67.
12. *"Sabbe dhammā anattā ti, yadā pannaya passati"*, - *Khuddakanikāya*, Vol. I, p. 43.
13. *"Tasmim kho pana samaye dhammā honti"* — *Dhammasangani* (Ed.) Bhikkhu J. Kashyap, Nalanda Edition, p. 37.
14. *"Manopubbangamā dhammā, manoseṭṭhā manomaya"* — *Khuddakanikāya*, Vol. I, p. 17.
15. *"Tattha Vuttābhidhammatthā catudhā paramatthato. Cittaṃ cetasikaṃ rupaṃ nibbānamiti sabbathā"* — *Abhidhammatthasangaho* (Ed.) Revatadharma, Varanasi, p. 1.
16. *Majjhimanikāya*, Vol. II, p. 373.
17. *Vibhanga*, (Ed.) Bhikkhu J. Kashyap, Nalanda Edition, p. 85.
18. *Samyuttanikāya*, Vol. IV, (Ed.) Bhikkhu J. Kashyap, Nalanda Edition, p. 373.
19. *Dīghanikāya*, Vol. II, Bhikkhu J. Kashyap, Nalanda, 1958, pp. 217-233.
20. *"Jāti pi dukkha, jarā pi dukkhā, maranaṃ pi dukkhaṃ — sankhittena pancupādānakkhandhā dukkhā"*- *Vibhanga*, p. 126.
21. *Vibhanga-aṭṭhakathā (Sammohavinodani)*, p. 84.
22. *Ibid.*, p. 85.
23. *"ettha hi bādhanalakkhanaṃ dukkhasaccaṃ, santāpanarasaṃ, pavatti paccupaṭṭhānam"* —*Ibid.*, p.86.
24. *Sammohavinodani*, p. 86.
25. *Ibid.*, p. 96.

26. *Ibid.*
27. *Dīghanikāya* II, p. 228; *Majjhimanikāya,* I, p. 67.
28. *Ibid.*
29. *'ya tesaṃ tesaṃ sattānaṃ tamhi tamhi sattanikāye jarā jiranatā, khandiccam pāliccam valittacatā āyuno sanhāni indriyānam paripāko ayam vuccati jarā — Vibhaṇga,* p. 126.
30. *'sā panesā khandhaparipākalakkhanā, maranupanayanarasā, yobbanavināsapaccupatthāna'-Sammohavinodani,* p. 101.
31. *"yā tesaṃ sattānaṃ tamhā tamhā sattanikāya cuti cavanatā bhedo antaradhānam muccu kālakiriyā khandhānam bhedo kalevarassa nikkhepā jivitindriyassupacehedoidaṃ vuccati maranaṃ" — Vibhaṇga,* p. 127.; *Dīghanikāya,* Vol. II, p. 228.
32. *Ibid.*
33. *Ibid.*
34. *Ibid.*
35. *Sammohavinodani,* p. 107.
36. *Therigāthā-aṭṭhakathā,* p. 225.
37. *Aṇguttaranikāya,* Vol. III, p. 30.
38. *Majjhimanikāya,* Vol. I, 6, p. 184.
39. *Mahāvaggo* (Ed.) Bhiikkhu J. Kashyap, Nalanda Edition, p. 14.

Buddhism Has Solutions from Suffering

14

Bela Bhattacharya

Every human being in this world wants peace, harmony and happiness. He does not want any kind of suffering. It is clear from the past till now. If we examine the present day situations in the family, society, nation and the world, then we will find the same situation. Each person is struggling hard to exploit the other. Each nation is also eager to dominate the weaker one. All these are the results of bloodshed, turmoil and distress all over the world. The peace of each individual and the nation is disturbed. If we try to examine the main causes of all this carefully it will be revealed that ignorance and craving are the root causes of all this. Ignorance (Avijja) is the non-comprehension of the Four Noble Truths of suffering, (dukkha), the causes of suffering (dukkhasamudaya), the cessation of suffering (dukkha-nirodha), and the path that leads to the cessation of suffering (dukkha-nirodha-gāminī patipadā).

The Buddha discovered the theory of the Four Noble Truths (Cattari Ariya Saccani) more than 2500 years ago. He arrived in this world with his message of non-violence (Ahimsa), compassion (Karuna), love (Metta), attitude to all mankind as of equal value, a casteless society and service to humanity.

Gautama Buddha went to Isipatana, Migadāya (Modern-Sarnath) near Varanasi soon after his Enlightenment at Bodhgaya and preached his first Sermon entitled "Dhamma-Cakka-Pavattana-Sutta" the Turning of the wheel of law, which contains the ethical code and philosophical tenets to his first disciples called Pancavaggiya-Bhikkhus. There he said to his disciples, "Go now and wander for the good of the many, for the happiness of the many". He also preached his doctrine which is glorious in the beginning, in the middle and in the end. "(Caratha Bhikkhave Cārikan bahujana hitāya, bahujana sukhāya, attāya hitāya, ca deva manussānam" — O Bhikkhus, go on with your rounds everywhere for the purpose of welfare to many, happiness to many and for the prosperity of many and the well-being of gods and mankind. This statement reveals the Buddha's philanthropic attitude towards mankind. In this historic Sermon he further spoke of the way which leads to remove sorrow, the Middlepath (Majjhima patipadā) and the Noble Eight-fold Path (Ariya-Atthan-gika-magga) to be the highest good in human life, viz., right view (sammā diṭṭhi), right thought (sammā-saṇkappa), right speech (sammā-vaca), right action (sāmma Kammanta), right livelihood (sammā-ajiva), right effort (sammāVāyāma), right mindfulness (sammā-sati), right concentration (sammāsamādhi). He renounced the worldly life to know the causes of human sufferings. He profoundly established his law of causation (Pāticca-samappāda) with momentariness (Khaṇikavāda). This law of dependent origination is regarded as one of the fundamental principles of Buddhism. The basic formula of this causal law is laid down in the Buddhist texts thus: This being, that becomes; from the arising of this, that arises; this not becoming, that does not become; from the ceasing of this, that ceases,[1] (Imasmin sati, idam hoti, imassuppādā, idam uppajjati, imasmin asati, idam na hoti, imassa nirodha, idam nirujjhati)[2].

According to Buddhism, the first Noble Truth is suffering. There is only one problem in this world, that is suffering. The world is full of suffering. According to the Buddha, the world is established on suffering, is founded on suffering[3]. Everything is bound by suffering, unsatisfactoriness, conflict — conflict between our desires and the facts of life. Every person is living in the world of problems and sufferings. The problems of food and clothing, the problems of shelter, the problems of our social life and surroundings are confronting us continuously, and at every moment many new problems are cropping up before us in some form or other as we see for ourselves.

Things which are transient are suffering. Whatever is impermanent is suffering[4]. "All created things are sorrowful, when one by wisdom realizes (this) he heeds not (is superior to) this world of sorrow, this is the path to purity"[5].

Suffering arises in men when he is faced with the facts of life such as ageing, illness, death and so forth. Vibhanga tells us, "Birth is suffering, ageing is suffering, death is suffering, sorrow, lamentation, pain (physical and mental) despair is suffering, association with the disliked is suffering, separation from the liked is suffering, not to get what one wishes that also is suffering, in brief the five aggregates (as objects of the attachments) are suffering"[6]. Birth is the existence and the appearance of the aggregates. Ageing means decrepitude, broken teeth, grey-hair, wrinkled skin, the dwindling of life, decay of the controlling faculties. Death is the breaking up of the aggregates, the destruction of the controlling faculty of the vital principle. Sorrow is the burning of the mind, mental pain. Lamentation is the senseless talk, wailing sorrowful murmuring. Pain may be physical and mental. Physical pain is the uneasy painful feeling born of bodily contact. Mental pain is the uneasy painful feeling born of mental contact. Despair is the state of despondency. The five aggregates are the attachments of suffering.

Having seen a sick man it is essential to discover the cause of his disease. The Buddha points out the causes of suffering and thus suggests the administration of a cure. Buddhism has searched into the sources and origins of suffering. The Cessation of suffering is known as Nibbana. It is the path of absolute ending of suffering. Buddhism has discovered the cure of this human malady, since the sufferings are absolutely manmade and the problems are created by man. The Cessation of suffering is the entire dispassionate cessation of the forsaking of, the discarding of, the freedom from, the non-attachment to that same craving. It is clear that nirodha means Nibbana which is the cessation, the extinction of craving or the extinction of suffering. Nirodha is the way of careful cultivation of the mind and produces unalloyed happiness and supreme rest from life.

The fourth Noble Truth is the path leading to the cessation of suffering. The path consists of eight good practices as mentioned before. This truth deals with the mental training of a man. It is a path leading to moral training. It is meditation or the development of the mind. It helps to improve the process of cleansing one's speech, action and thought. It is the path which leads to a man for self-development and self-purification. It indicates a man progressing from ignorance to full knowledge. The eight-fold path may be divided into three sections, 1. moral precepts (sila), 2. mind control (Samadhi) and 3. wisdom (panna). These are held as the three-fold training. These three are inter-related. They can't go alone. They go together supporting each other. The moral precepts strengthen meditation which promotes wisdom. Wisdom helps one to be free from ignorance. Thus one can clean one's speech, action and thought.

The third truth is the cessation of Samsara. So is the path, the last and the fourth truth the Noble-Eight-fold path. It raises a man from lower to higher levels of existence. It leads a man from darkness to light, from passion to a passionless stage. It indicates the path to purification and deliverance. It aims at the highest purification, perfect mental health. It is a must for the spiritual uplift of the mind of a man. Nibbana is the goal for deliverance from bondage. Nibbana is a stage which can be realized through supreme knowledge. In the state of Nibbana one can be free from the bondages of past deeds. It is indeed a noble conception. It is free from all kinds of bondages. It is the ultimate goal of all Buddhists. It is the end of misery produced by birth, disease, old age and the chain of rebirth. It is the goal of the spiritual pilgrimage. Really, it is the state of perfect calmness and tranquillity. All desires for this life and the next are extinguished on its attainment. It is the ideal, the highest good and the summum bonum of life. So we can conclude that Buddhism has solutions for sufferings.

So the greatness of the Buddha is for his two-fold attitude, one for his leading man to eradicate sorrow by living an ideal life in accordance with the middle path, and the other for his ahimsa non-Violence, friendliness (metta), Karuna sympathy which are conducive to bring about world peace and harmony.

References

1. Pali Dictionary, Rhys Davids, page, 394.

2. Samyutta-Nikāya, P.T.S. Vol-II, pages 28, 65, 95, 96; Majjhima-Nikāya, P.T.S. Vol. II, page, 32; Vol-1, 262, Vol-III, 63; Udāna — R. Samkrityayana (Nagari), Suttas -1-2; Abhidharma-Kosa, Vol. II, pp — 81-83 (which discusses the significance of saying separately "Asmim sati..." And "Imassa uppādā..."); Mūamadhymaka-Kārikā-1, p. 55.

3. 'Dukkhe loko patitthito'. Samyutta-Nikāya — 1, p. 40.

4. 'Yad aniccam tam dukkham'. Samyutta-Nikāya, P.T.S. Vol, III, p. 22.

5. "Sabhe saṇkhāra dukkhā,
ti yadā paṇṇāya passati
atha nibbindati dukkhe,
esa maggo visuddhiyā."
The Dhammapada, Verse, 278.

6. The Book of Analysis — Pathamakyaw Ashim Thittila (Setthila) Aggamaha Pandita, p. 130 "Jāti pi dukkhā, jarā pi dukkhā, maranam pi dukkham, sokaparideva-dukkha domanassupāyāsā pi dukkhā, appiyehi sampayogo dukkho, piyehi vippayogo dukkho, yaṃ picchaṃ na labhati tam pi dukkham, saṃkhittena pancupadana-kkhandhā dukkhā". Vibhanga Pali, Saccavibhanga, Bhikkhu Jagadish Kassapa, p. 126.

Buddhist View of Suffering as discussed in Abhidharmakośa of Vasubandhu in Sarvāstivāda School

15

Narendra Kumar Dash

"चिरं तिट्ठतु सद्धम्मो
दुःख अरियसच्चं (दुःख आर्यसत्यं)

I quote the *Buddhavacana-*

"There are two things, o monks, which make the truth-based Dhàmma endure for a long time, without any distortion and without (fear of) eclipse,. Which two? Proper placement of words and their natural interpretation."

द्वेमे भिक्खवे, धम्मा
सद्धम्मस्य ठितिया असम्मोसाय अनन्तरधानाय संवत्तन्ति। कतमे द्वे सुनिक्खत्त-ञ्च पदभ्यञ्जनं अत्थो च सुनीतो। सुनिक्खित्तस्स, भिक्खवे पदभ्यञ्जनस्स अत्थोपि सुनयो होति ।। (अ . नि . दुक्खनिपातं 21)

At the outset, there should be clarity while discussing any aspect of doctrine as in *nikāyās* which are found in Pali Language and the same aspect of doctrine discussed in the scriptures (*āgamas*) belonging to the *Sarvāstivāda* school of Buddhist thought expressed either in hybrid Sanskrit or Prakṛt or in Sanskrit. The tradition accepts from the historical point of view that there are two main schools of thought as 'original Buddhism' and the other as Developed Buddhism.

From the history of Buddhism in India, we know that, after the Buddha obtained perfect enlightenment, he began to preach for the salvation of all human beings (सर्वमुक्ति अट्ठदीपो) to carry out his purpose. After due delīberation, the Buddha preached for a pretty long period of 45 years (530 B.C.- 486 B.C.), beginning from the first sermon at the Deer-Park near Banaras, known as **'Dhammacakka-Pavattana Sutta"** (which is generally mentioned as such in the **Aṭṭhakathā** or in the **Vinayapiṭaka**) and ending with the teaching embodied in the **Mahāparinibbāna Sutta** at Kuśinara. During these years, as far as history records, he preached and explained only his doctrine of phenomenological perceptions with the 'Four Noble Truths' (चत्तारि-अरियसच्चानि) (चत्वारि-आर्य-सत्यानि) as its basis namely (i) Suffering (दु:ख) by which he used to explain the question of 'the what' of the apparent world, (2) Its cause (दु:खसमुदय) by which he used to answer the question of 'why', 'how" of the same Samsāra (3) 'suppression' (दु:खनिरोध) and (4) the path leading to its final extinction (दु:खनिरोधमार्ग). Besides these, we have two other formulae embodying the Buddha's instruction : (i) The three fold corner stone of Buddhism, viz., 'All is impermanent, सब्ब अनिच्चं) (सर्व अनित्यं) 'All is suffering' (सब्बं दुक्खं) (सर्व दु:ख) and 'All is ego-less/without self' (सब्बा अनत्ता) सर्वा अनात्मा).

(ii) The famous term 'twelve linked chain of causation' (द्वादश पटिच्चसमुत्पन्न) (द्वादश प्रतीत्यसमुत्पाद). The former is a minute explanation of 'Duhkkha' and the latter is a minute statement of *'Dukkha Samudaya'*. However, the fact that occurs to us is that, all throughout, the Buddha never preached his introspectional Ontological Doctrine explicitly. The reason for this, according to my opinion, is that he always considered the capacity and the necessity of the people around him, so that he preached whatever was useful and apt to suit the particular conditon and environment, religious, philosophical and social of that age. We should not forget the most important feature of the Buddha's preaching that he always considered the time, the place, the person, and the totality of these circumstances, whenever, whatever and to whomsoever he was going to preach-

तथागतो अरहं सम्मासम्बुद्धो अत्थञ्ञू, धम्माञ्ञू
मत्ताञ्ञू, कालाञ्ञू, परिसञ्ञू .. इमेहि पञ्चहि

धम्मेहि समन्नागतो तथागतो. धम्मेनेव अनुत्तरं
धम्मचक्कं पवत्तेति (A.N.V.p.131).

- "The noble Tathāgata, the perfectly Awakened one, knows the sense, the **Dhamma**, the proportion, the time, the assembly. Endowed with these five qualities Tathāgata turns the transcendental Wheel of the Law according to the **Dhamma**." If this is kept in mind, then the understanding of बुद्धवचन as in *nikāyas* and the same as elucidated in the later school could be understood well.

"..................the **Dhamma** (truths) which ' I have taught to you after realizing with my super-knowledge, should be recited by all, in concert and without dissension, in a uniform version collating meaning with meaning and wording with wording. In this way, this teaching with pure practice will last long and endure for a long time.

- ये वो मया धम्मा अभिञ्ञा देसिता, तत्थ सब्बेव सङ्गम्म अत्थेन अत्थं भ्यञ्जनेन भ्यञ्जनं सङ्गायितब्बं न विवदितब्बं यथयिदं ब्रह्मचरियं अद्धनियं अस्स चिरट्ठितिकम (D.N.3. पासादिकसुत्त 177)

Thus the बुद्धवचन of sixth century B.C. were preserved and endured with philosophical and anthropological significance by his followers- the Buddhist philosophers of 5th Century A.D. like Asanga, Vasubandhu, Dinnāga and Dharmakīrti. Although each one of them sought to reinterpret the Buddha's thoughts yet each retained the basic principle. When Vasubandhu tried to reinterpret the Buddha's thoughts, he stressed the point to solve human problems, hence instead of advocating and formulating any methodology, he interpreted human nature and his action in the light of the Buddha's teaching. While solving problems of human suffering the Budha advocated the above four Noble Truths. Vasubandhu in his Abhidharmakośa and Kośabhāsya related these truths with man and his action and tried to give practical acceptability to the Buddha's teaching.

Vasubandhu's View of Dukkha (Sarvāstivāda view)

One may understand the term दुक्ख / दुःख as grief or pain but however it leads to the experience of suffering only. Now I quote Vasubandhu's view. Can I refer to him as the view of Sarvāstivāda? The sixth Kośasthāna begins with the discussion that the defilements are abandoned through Seeing the Truths and through Meditation. In this contest vasubandhu mentions the Four Truths—the order of these truths so as to be comprehended (अभिसमय) **(i)** Why are they to be comprehended in this order? because, in the period preparatory to the path proper, that is, the period of examination, the ascetic first creates an idea of that to which he is attached, of that by which he is tormented, of that from which he seeks to be delivered, namely suffering- यत्र हि सक्तो येन च बाध्यते यतश्च, मो ब्रं प्रार्थयते, तदेवादौ व्यवचारणावस्थायां दुःखसत्यं परीक्षयते। [*Abhidharma Kośa* VI.p. 68.7] पञ्चात् कोऽस्य हेतुरिति समुदयसत्यं, कोऽस्य निरोध सत्यं, कोऽस्य मार्ग इति मार्गसत्यम्। व्याधिं दृष्ट्वा तन्निदानदायभेषजान्वेषणवत् ।। -"Then he asks what is its cause, and he created an idea of the origin. Then he asks what does extinction consist of, and he creates an idea of extinction. Then he asks what is the Path of extinction, and he created an idea of the Path. So too having seen a disease, one searches out its origin, its disappearance, and its remedy."

Before going into the details on the discussion of these 'Four Noble Truths', Abhidharmakośa begins with the question as to why the term 'Arya' is used for these four Truths. Because they are the truths of the *Āryans*. Does this mean that they are false for the non-*Āryans*? Not being erroneous, they are true for everyone. But the *Āryans* see them as they are, that is to say-they see suffering-the *upādhānaskandhas* as suffering, impermanent etc... others do not. Therefore the truths are called "Truths of the Aryans" and not truths of others because the seeing of these latter is incorrect-"What the Aryans call happy (i.e. *Nirvāṇa*) others call painful; what others call happy, the Āryans call painful-"

यदार्थाः सुखतः प्राहुस्तत् परे दुःखतो विदुः ।
यद् परे सुखतः प्राहुस्तदार्या दुःखतो विदुः ।। गाथा (2)

It is further questioned-since only a part of sensation (वेदना) is painful by its nature,how can one say that all impure, conditioned things are suffering? There are three types of suffering - suffering which is suffering in and of itself (दु:खदु:खता), suffering which changes cr transforms (विपरिणामदु:खता) and suffering through the fact of being conditioned (संसकादु:खता). By reason of these three, all impure conditioned things, without exception, are suffering - agreeable things are suffering in and of themselves; and neither disagreeable- nor agreeable things are suffering because they are conditioned. What are the agreeable *dharmas*? The three sensations, all the *Samskāras* which result in agreeable sensation, etc... receive the name of agreeable, etc..

The agreeable sensation is suffering through transormation as the sūtra says, 'Agreeable sensation is agreeable when it arises, agreeable when it lasts, but suffering in its change". Disagreeable sensation is suffering by nature - "suffering sensation is suffering when it arises, and suffering while it lasts. Neither arises, and suffering while it lasts. Neither disagreeable-nor disagreeable sensation is suffering because it is so decreed by its causes, that which is impermanent is suffering"-प्रत्ययाभिसंस्कारणादि यद् अनित्यं तद् दु:खम् ।) Thus all conditioned things are suffering from the fact of suffering through the fact of being conditioned, and they are seen under this aspect only by the Āryans-

ऊर्णपक्ष यथैव हि करतलसंस्थं न वेद्यते पुम्भिः ।
अक्षिगतं तु तथैव हि जनयत्यरतिं च पीडां च ॥
खकरतलसदृशो बालो न वेत्ति संस्कारदु : खतापदम।
अक्षिसदृशस्तु विद्वांस्तेनैवोद्वेज्यते गाढम् ॥ इति-

"One does not feel a hair placed on the palm of the hand, but the same hair, in the eye, causes suffering and injury. So too the ignorant, resembling that hand, do not feel the hair which is suffering through the fact of being conditioned; but the Aryans, resembling the eye, are tortured by it". (*ibid*.p.689). One may further question here that the Path is conditioned; it should thus be suffering from the fact of suffering through the fact of being conditioned. It is explained that the path is not suffering, because the definition of suffering is to be hateful. Now the Path is not hateful to the Aryans because it produces the extinction of all the sufferings of arising; when they consider Nirvāṇa, as peaceful, what they consider as peaceful, is the extinction of what they consider as suffering (namely impure conditioned things, and not the extinction of the path).

प्रतिकूलं हि दुःखमितिलक्षणान्नं मार्गो दुःखम्। यदा आर्याः निर्वाणं शान्ततः पश्यन्ति, तदपि यदेव दुःखतः दृष्टं तस्यैव निरोधं शान्ततः पश्यान्तं न मार्गस्य)

But, since the agreeable or happiness does not exist, why are only sufferings and not the agreeable, a truth of the Aryans? (1) According to one explanation, it is because of the slightness of happiness. In the same way that one calls a pile in which some peas are to be found, a pile of beans," so too no one with any intelligence would consider a wound as agreeable because one experiences a very small agreeable sensation when one washes one's wound. (2) And further, because it is a cause of suffering because it is produced by many sufferings, because one desires it when one suffers, the agreeable, they conclude, is suffering". (3) But, even if accompanied by happiness, existence in its totality has the same flavour of suffering through the fact of being conditioned: the Aryans consider these as suffering. This is why suffering and not happiness is an *Aryan* Truth.

To sum up, Vasubandhu quoting the Buddha's view accepts *'Dukkha'* as the first in the order of the 'Four Āryasatya-s' because we experience *'Dukkha'* first, then we think about its causes; hence *'Dukkha Kāraṇa'* comes second. After understanding the causes of suffering, we attempt to overcome this suffering and then realize that *'Dukkha Nirodha'* is possible. And by following *'Dukkha Nirodhamārga'*, we attain the *'Nirvāṇa'*. In this way Vasubandhu justifies the sequence of the order and the reason for using the term *'Ārya'* in *'Ārya Satyas', (Abhidharmakośa*, VI.p.689). This shows that, according to Vasubandhu, the sequence of realization of the 'Four Āryasatyas' is determined by the experience of an individual on the one hand, and his capacity of reasoning on the other.

According to Vasubandhu *Tṛṣṇā*, *Avidyā* and *karma* are the three causes of suffering (कर्म च तृष्णा च अथो अविद्या संस्कारणं हेतुरतिसम्पराये, *ibid*.p.397). Generally it is the tendency or desire of man to do certain things or to perform an action in order to get more and more pleasure. It is this desire which can roughly be called as *Tṛṣṇā*. It is only thirst or desire or greed (तन्हा = तृष्णा) that is the origin of suffering. *Tṛṣṇā* is defined as '*Nandīrāga* ˁ.*nagatā*" (*Mahāvagga* i.6.20; समुदयसत्यं कतमात्य यासौ तृष्णा न..ागसहगता तत्र तत्राभिनन्दिनी।).

When the Buddha said, 'it is desire which is the origin', he intedend to define the cause of reexistence (अभिनिवृत्ति). He enumerates action, desire, and ignorance; he defined the cause of different births (उपपत्ति) which is action; the cause of the re-existence, namely desire; (गाथायं अभिनिवृत्ति हेतुं ब्रुवता समुदयसत्यं तृष्णा ए उद्रफ) and the cause of births and of re-existence namely ignorance. ("कर्महेतु : उपपत्तये, तुष्णा हेतुः अभिनिर्वृत्तये इति स्त्रत्रोत्रातु) i.e. the action is the cause of births, and desire is the cause of re-existence and it teaches the successive order of causation. The eye has action for its object, action has desire for its cause; desire has ignorance for its cause; and ignorance has incorrect judgment for its cause". That consciousness and the other *skandhas* are the origin of suffering results again from the fact that they are respectively seed and field-(सहेतु सप्रत्यसनिदानसूत्रे क्रमेण वा बीजक्षेत्रभावं प्रतिपादयता विज्ञानदयोऽत्युक्ता:)

Now it is questioned 'का पुनरुपपत्तिः का चाभिनिवृत्तिः ? what is birth (उपपत्ति) ? What is re-existence (अभिनिर्वृत्ति) ? "*Upapatti*" signifies a birth or an existence characterized by a certain sphere (कामधातु etc..), a certain reality of rebirth (god, human, etc..) a certain mode of birth (from a womb, from an egg etc..) a certain gender, etc. (धातुगतियोन्यादि प्रकारभेदनात्मभावस्योपपदनमुपपत्तिः) *Abhinirvṛtti* signifies re-existence without qualification (अभेदेन पुनर्भवप्रतिसन्धानमभिनिर्वृत्तिः) The cause of birth is action and the cause of re-existence is desire; so too a seed is the cause of a shoot characterized as a rice-shoot, wheat-shoot, etc.. whereas water in the cause of the simple germination of all the different species of shoots. (तयोर्यथाक्रमं कर्म च भवतृष्णा च हेतुः। तद्यथा बीजं शालियवादि जातिप्रकार भेदेनाङ्कुरोपपादनस्य हेतुः । आपः पुनरभेदेन सर्वाङ्कुरप्ररोह मात्रस्य –इत्येव दृष्टान्तः) How does one prove that desire is the cause of re-existence?

From the fact that a person free from desire is not re-born. When a person endowed with desire and a person free from desire die, we know that the first is reborn and that the second is not reborn. Thus there is no rebith where there is no desire, we know that desire is the cause of re-existence. "तृष्णा अभिनिर्वृत्तिहेतुरिति कात्र युक्तिः

वीततृष्णस्यजन्माभावात् । उभयेऽमि म्रियन्ते सतृष्णा वीततृष्णाश्च । सतृष्णा एव जाता दृश्यन्ते, न वीततृष्णा इति; विना तृष्णया जन्माभावात् ।

Vasubandhu refers to three types of greed or desire (तृष्णा) viz., *Kāma tṛṣṇā, Rūpa tṛṣṇā* and *Arūpa tṛṣṇā-* यो लोभः स तृष्णा पीड़ितः वित्तिः प्राक् भोगमैथुनरागिणः। उपादानं तु भोगानां प्राप्तये परिधावतः) This kind of Tṛṣṇā gives rise to three kinds of Dukkha; viz., Dukkhadukkhatā, Samskakāra, Duhkhatā, Vipariṇāma Dukkhatā.

What is this *Dukkha Dukkhatā*? All types of mental and physical sufferings are named as Dukkhadukkhatā (eg.) old age, diseases, etc..

What is *Samskāra Dukkhatā*? According to Vasubandhu everything in the world is momentary and constantly changing. Human being is not an exception to this. He is also momentary. However due to avidyā or ignorance a man cannot realize this and attempts to indulge himself and becomes unhappy. Hence, the structure of human being which is called as *upādāna skandha* is Duhkhakāraka. This type of suffering which arises due to *upadāna skanda* is named *samskāra Duhkhatā.*

Vipariṇāma Duhkhatā: According to Vasubandhu everything in the world is changing and momentary so also pleasure is also changing. But a man having ignorance fails to realize this and becomes unhappy after achieving the pleasure sought by him. This type of suffering which is the result of instability of man is *Vipariṇāma Duhkhatā.*

Duhkha samudesya as the second Āryasatya:

Vasubandhu explains and elaborates the cause of suffering by advocating the doctrine of *Prātityasamuthāda.* According to him, in the origin of suffering there are twelve links. These links are interdependent as their coming into existence is dependent on others. These twelve links are as follows:

Avidyā, saṃskāra, vijñāna, nāma-rūpa, ṣaḍāyatana, sparśa, vedanā, tṛṣṇā upadāna, bhāva, jāti, jarā and maraṇa.-

Duhkhanirodha as a third Āryasatya:

According to this Āryasatya, Duhkha is not necessary for an individual to take next birth. By following the way suggested by the Buddha an individual is able to attain the Nirvāṇa. *Duhkha nirodhagamini Pratipad* as a fourth Ārya satya: Pratipad means a way or Path. The way of removing *Duhkha* and of leading to *Nirvāṇa is Duhkha Nirodhagāmini Pratipad.*

According to Vasubandhu, human action has an important role to play in the creation of suffering as well as in the attainment of *Nirvāṇa.* Because, as Vasubandhu believes, human action is the reflection of human mind, it is governed and determined by the desires, and thoughts of man. There is a consistency in his thought and action. Hence, when a man having *Tṛṣṇā* performs an action, it gives suffering to that man as well as to other men. Similarly when a man having no *Tṛṣṇā* performs an action, it does not give suffering to him as well as to the other men. Thus Vasubandhu believes that there is a relation between thought and action.

When he talks about *Duhkha Nirodhagāmini Pratipad*, he elaborates this path in such a way that there will be a consistency in thought and action. In order to serve this purpose, at first he suggests how human mind and thought will become free from *Tṛṣṇā* and afterwards he suggests how this thought which is without *Tṛṣṇā* will be reflected in man's bodily action and in his speech.

Vasubandhu defines *Duhkha Nirodhagāmini Pratipad*, as an appropriate path for *Duhkha Nirodha* as it is conducive to *Duhkha Nirodha* and it also helps the individual to attain the Nirvāṇa. He believes that if an individual follows this path, then he will be in a position to face the problem of suffering.

In other words it could be said that *Duhkha Nirodhagāmini Pratipad* is a kind of discipline which disciplines the individual in order to become moral in his thought and action.

This *Duhkha Nirodhagāmini Pratipad* is eightfold:

1. *Samyak Dṛṣti* is right knowledge of four *Ārya satya*, Dharma and principles of *Anityatā, Anātma and suffering*.

2. *Samyak sankalpa* is right apprehension or thought of man due to which man becomes without having *Tṛṣṇa* or feelings.
3. *Samyak vac* is right speech whichk means man's refraining from lying, backbiting, harsh talk, and idle gossip. It is the connecting link between thought and action.
4. *Samyak karma* is right action which consists of *Pañca śila*, namely, not to kill, not to take that which is not given; not to commit sexual misconduct; not to indulge in false speech and not to partake of intoxicating drinks.
5. *Samyak Ajīvika* is right livelihood. According to *samyak Ajīvika*, an individual does not perform those actions for his livelihood that are harmful to others.
6. *Samyak vyāyāma* is right effort of man for self-perfection. Man makes effort for self-perfection by avoiding bad qulities and by acquiring good qualities.
7. *Samyak smṛti* is right memory of man being aware of his body, feeling and mind.
8. *Samyak samādhi* is right concentration.

If we go through the perceptives of Vasubandhu on human suffering, we will find that Vasubandhu attempts to relate human suffering and its emancipation to the nature of man and his action. He believes that, if man realizes that he has certain qualities and capacities, then he can easily control his qualities and action and thereby eradicate suffering.

Suffering as Expounded by Early Disciples of Buddha

16

Meena V. Talim

In the present paper I have selected some of the monks from Theragāthā and nuns from Therigāthā who will explain their versions of 'Dukkha'- Suffering. The purpose of choosing these two books is to get first-hand information from their auto-biographical verses. Besides, most of these monks and nuns were contemporary to the Buddha. Dr. Winternitz has pointed out that these gāthās were not collected and carefuly preserved during Gotama's life- time and soberly fixed soon after his death.[1] One may accept that they may have been fixed between third cent. B.C. as an upper limit and 1st Century B.C. as a lower limit; at the time of King Vaṭṭagāmini when the Pali-cannon came into writing, in 1st Century B.C.[2] We will study another book, named "*Miliñda-Pañho*" (1st Century A.D.) for this topic. This is a non-canonical book which contains the views of a lay-follower and a monk on this subject. Thus these books are more or less contemporary to each other but with different backgrounds and substances.

Therigāthā narrates diiferent layers of the mundane sufferings of women. In the words of Kisāgotami "दुक्खो इत्थिभावो" - womanhood is suffering ! She talks about the pains and agony that a woman has to go through while giving birth to a child. She remembers how after the death of her only child she ran into the city to get mustard seed from a house where no death has ever occurred. Soṇā, an elderly nun, speaks about the sorrows of a mother. She had looked after her ten children well; after the renunciation of her husband she distributed all wealth to them, keeping nothing for herself but in her old age they discarded her. Isidāsi remembers the sad experiences of her married life. She served her husbands* as a dāsi would do but in spite of such humiliation her marriages were broken. Ambāpāli, the courtesan of Vesāli, realizes the transitory element of the body, on the factual basis of human phenomena, but her agony is evident. Chāpā, a rustic, mischievous and jolly maiden, is not able to understand the intellectual level of her husband, who in the end leaves her. Bhaddākuṇḍala-kesā, a young and innocent girl, fell in love with a wicked and shrewd dacoit who tramples down her love. Patācāra, a daughter of a merchant, elopes with a servant working in the house and suffers throughout her life. All these nuns talk about their bitter experiences of lives and mention them 'As a dart of sorrow that had pierced my heart' (सल्लं मे हदयनिस्सितं ।) .

One cannot scoff at these feminine experiences as personal tragedies but should know that these are the facts of a woman's life. In modern generation too one can find many women suffering more or less in similar situations; only the labels are different. It means that the category of a woman's sufferings-*Dukkha-* is different that that of a man. It is more related to psychological factors.

In *Therigāthā* we see different shades and tinges of sorrow which are eternal factors of womanhood. However from her ego-centric sorrow the nun attempted to focus on the broader universal truth. From the mundane layers of sufferings, the nun successfully emerged to transcendental stratum. In this process of development we do not see the nuns as enthusiastic as the monks. Why? Her task, to me, is more difficult than that of a monk, as first she has to cut off the ties of emotions, penetrate into oblivion, grasp the spiritual tenets and adopt them faithfully. This long procedure of stabilization made her fatigued and therefore she is less eloquent than a monk, in expressing her achivements. The verses of the nuns are therefore more subdued.

The intensity of her personal sorrow made the nun more understanding and analytical. She is perceptible to three dogmas, namely *Dukkha*, *Anattā* and *Aniccatā*. She found solutions to get rid of Dukkha in Buddha's teachings. However the ways of handling them are different from those of the monks. Most of these nuns have found different ways to overcome *Dukkha*. Some say that 'I went into seclusion (एकमन्तं उपाविसिं)[3]. Some say that they meditated in the night and "I entered into Vihāra holding a lamp in my hand, I sat and cleaned the wick of the lamp and concentrated on the lamp. My mind became free and I obtained nibbāṇa"[5]. The nun Mahāpajāpati Gotami said, "I have realized the cause of *Dukkha* whereby all cravings in me have dried up. I have followed the eightfold noble path and touched the path of cessations"[6].

Let us study some of the verses of the nuns that would give us an idea about their struggle to win over Dukkha:-

Sāmā and Abhayā nuns say:-

बहूहि दुक्खधम्मेहि अप्पमादरताय मे ।
तण्हक्खयो अनुप्पत्तो कतं बुध्दस्स सासनं ।।[7]

I have been watchful towards the constituents of Dukkha.

I have obtained cessation of craving by following the teachings of the Buddha.

Sujātā Theri says:-

सुत्वा च महेसिस्स सच्चं सम्पटिविज्झ हं।
तत्थे'व विरजं धम्मं फुसयिं अमतं पदं ।। 1 ।।

ततो विञ्ञातसध्दम्मा पब्बजिं अनगारिमं ।
तिस्सो विज्ञा अनुप्पत्ता अमोघं बुध्दसासनं ।। 2 ।।[8]

I have followed the four-noble truths, after hearing the great sage;

There only have I touched the peerless norm and obtained a state of nectar // 1 //

Then, knowing the good law, I have renounced and entered into the houseless state;

I have obtained three knowledges and followed the teachings of the Buddha, the wise-one // 2 //

Guttā Theri says:__

रागं मानं अविज्जञ्च उध्दच्चञ्च विवज्जिय ।
संयोजनानि छेत्वानं दुक्खस्स' न्तं करिस्ससि ।। 1 ।। [9]

Discard lust, pride, ignorance and excitement. By cutting all these bondages one can end *Dukkha.*

Kisāgotami Theri says:-

भवितो मे मग्गो अरियो अट्ठङ्गिको अमतगामी।
निब्बाणं सच्छिकतं धम्मदासं अपेकिख' हं।। १ ।।
अहम 'म्हि कन्तसल्ला ओहितभारा कतं में करणीयं।
किसागोतमी थेरी सुविभुत्तचित्ता इमं भणी' ति ।। २ ।।

I have cultivated the noble eight fold path that leads to immortality;

I have witnessed nibbāṇa (as clearly as) one sees oneself in a mirror

I, I am the one who has taken out the dart that had pierced my heart;

Discarded the burden, I did what had to be done,

Nun Kisagotami, whose mind is free, says this.

Rohiṇi Theeri says:-

सचे भायसि दुक्खस्स सचे ते दुक्खमप्पियं।
उपेहि बुध्दं सरणं धम्मदासं अपेकिख' हं ।। 1 ।।
अहम 'म्हि कन्तसल्ला ओहितभारा कतं मे करणीयं।
किसागोतमी थेरी सुविभुत्तचित्ता इमं भणी 'ति ।। 2 ।। [10]

Rohiṇi Theri says:-

सचे भायसि दुक्खस्स सचे ते दुक्खमप्पियं।
उपेहि बुध्दं सरणं धम्मं सङ्घञ्च तादिनं।
समादियाहि सीलानि तं ते अत्थाय होहिति ।। 1 ।।

If you are afraid of *Dukkha*, if you do not like *Dukkha*, then take refuge in Buddha, *Dhamma* and *Sangha*, observe the moral precepts which will be beneficial to you.

This is a direct appeal to those who are suffering.

Sihā Theri says:-

ततो रज्जुं गहेत्वान पाविसिं वनमन्तरं ।
वरं मे इध उब्बन्धं यञ्च हीनं पुना' चरे ।। 1 ।।

दळ्हं पासं करित्वान रुकरवसाखाय बन्धिय ।
पाकखिपिं पासं गीवाय अथ चित्तं विमुच्चि में ।। 2 ।। [12]

I entered the thicket of the forest, taking a rope with me. It is better here,to fasten myself than to lead a low life. Having tightened the noose I tied it to the branch of a tree. I threw the noose on my neck and that very moment my mind was released.

This is an example of a frustrated nun who tried to commit suicide. It shows how nuns struggled to reach the ultimate goal of the renunciated ones.

Unlike the monks, the nuns have more personal or internal (अज्झत्तिकानि) causes that made them to renounce the world. They are oppressed by these internal causes. In such a depressed state of minds they tried to find solace in renunciation. At the initial stage the nuns looked at *Dukkha* as a calamity. There is some sort of helplessness, exhaustion in their attitude. There is more of obedience; it is like a person who swallows bitter medicine to get well soon. At the training period they do not look as enthusiastic as the monks; but they made an earnest and desperate attempt to come out of *Dukkha*. They religiously followed the teachings of the Buddha the *Samatha* and *Vipassana* forms of meditation to obtain spiritual level. Thus we notice that there is a positive change in women. After receiving the training in the nunnery they have discarded *dukkha* completely. Each and every nun had to struggle independently to achieve emancipation without seeking help from their preceptors.

II

The monks do not narrate their personal sufferings- *Dukkha*, which they have taken as the facts of life. As I have pointed out before, we notice that there is a basic difference in the attitude of man and woman. Hence their levels of sufferings or struggle for conquering the sufferings are all different from those of the nuns. Therefore we observe that the monks are more open, daring and free in their verses. Let us study some of the verses.

Kātiyāna Thera Says:

उट्ठेहि निसदि कातियानच मा निद्दाबहुलो अहु, जागरस्सु ।

मा तं अलसं पमत्तबन्धु; कूटेने' व जिनातु मच्चुराजा ॥ 1 ॥

Get up Kātiyāna, do not sit; you have slept for a long time, get up;

Do not be lazy, oh imprudent monk;

You have to win over the bad one, the King of death.

सेय्यथापि महासमुद्दवेगो, एवं जातिजरावत्तते तं ।

सो करोहि सुदीपम त्तनो त्वं, न हि ताणं तव विज्जते' व अञ्ञं ॥ 2 ॥

Just as the great ocean with torrents of flood engulfs all,

Similarly birth and old age vanquishes all;

Therefore make an island for yourself.

There is no other refuge for you, than your own conquest.

These verses reveal the enthusiastic and conscientious attempt of a monk to overcome sufferings.

Nhātakamuni Thera says: [14]

पितिसुखेन विपुलेन फरित्वान समुस्सयं ।

लूखाम्पि अभिसम्भोन्तो विहारस्सामि कानने ॥ 1 ॥

भावेन्तो सत्त बोज्झङ्गे इन्द्रियानि बलानि च।

ज्ञानसुखमसम्पन्नो विहिरिस्सामं कानने ॥ 2 ॥

Though I am weak, I shall wander fearlessly in the forest, spreading around the happiness of love (i.e. Matta). // 1 //

I shall cultivate the seven factors of wisdom that would strengthen my sense organs,

I shall wander in the forest enjoying the bliss of meditation//2//

This monk though weak in body is strong in mind. His confidence overwhelms through his diction, as if he has found the key to get rid of *Dukkha*.

Upasena Vangantoputta Thero says:-[15]

न सो उपवदे कञ्चि उपघातं विवज्जये ।

संवुतो पातिमोक्खस्मिं, मतञ्ञू च' स्स भोजने ॥ 1 ॥

सुग्गहितनिमित्तस्स चित्तस्सु 'प्पादककोविदो ।

समथं अनुयुञ्जय्य कालेन च विपस्सनं ॥ 2 ॥

Do not retaliate or hurt any one by speech

Be restrainful, follow the *Pātimokkha* rules and be moderate in food // 1 //

Stick to the good objects of meditation and be master

Follow *Samatha* and gradually shift to Vipassanā // 2 //

This shows the experimental stages in the life of a monk who from simple disciplinary rule rises to master Vipassanā that ends the sufferings of human life.

Sāriputta Thero says:-

ना 'भिनन्दामि मरणं वा ना 'भिनन्दामि जीवितं ।

कालञ्च पटिकङ्खामि निब्बिसं भतको यथा ॥ 1 ॥

उभयेन इदं मरणे 'वा ना' मरणं पच्छा वा पुरे वा ।

पटिपज्जथ मा विनस्सथ, खणो मा उपच्चगा ॥ 2 ॥

I do not enjoy death nor do I enjoy life,

I think of time just as a labourer on wages craves for boiled rice

I have discarded the thought of death or no death whether at early age or later age

Follow this, do not destroy yourself, let not a moment go wasted.

Here monk Sāriputta gives importance to the time-factor and warns not to be too emotional about life and death. Every moment of life should be utilized to overcome sufferings- that is what he intends to tell us.

Tālaputta Thero says:-[17]

दुक्ख 'ति खन्धे पटिपस्स योनिसो ।

यतो च दुक्खं समुदेति तं जहं ॥

इधे 'व दुक्खस्स करोहि अन्तं।
इति' स्सु मं चित्तं पुरे नियुञ्जसि ।।

Dukkha consists of five elements that give rise to birth,/ Discard those causes of Dukkha / End Dukkha here (in this life) only, / This is what my mind had decided, long time ago.

A monk, here giving stress on the five elements of the senses and with determination, sees the end of suffering - दुक्ख

Pārāpariya Thero says:-[18]

इन्द्रियानि मनुस्सानं हिताय' हिताय च ।
अरक्खितानि अहिताय रक्खितानि हिताय च ।। 1 ।।

मनं चे 'तेहि धम्मेहि यो न सककोति राकखेतुं ।
ततो दुक्खम 'न्वेति सब्बेहे' तेहि पञ्चहि ।। 2 ।।

The Five sense organs of a man are meant for benefit and loss;

If they are not controlled, one is at a loss but when controlled one benefits // 1 //

All worldly phenomena arise through the mind which is difficult to control;

Thereby one suffers owing to these five elements // 2 //

A monk does not blame the sensory elements but feels that, when controlled, they are beneficial. He gives importance to the mind that can eventually end Dukkha.

Aññākoṇḍanñño Thero says:-[19]

सब्बे सङ्खारा अनिच्चा' ति यदा पञ्ञाय पस्सति ।
अथ निब्बन्दति दुक्खे, एत मग्गे विसुद्धिया ।।

When one realizes with wisdom that all component things are impermanent,

Then his sufferings will end, this is a path of purity.

A monk here gives more importance to wisdom (Paññā) and instructs that the process of getting rid of suffering passes through wisdom.

Thus we notice in all the above verses that the monks are enthusiastic and very optimistic about getting rid of sufferings. They recommend various ways to conquer *Dukkha* and reach *Nibbāṇa*. The monks look at suffering as a challenge and accept it boldly. They are cool and have nothing to grumble about their past lives. They are more attentive to Dukkha and analytical towards the Buddha's Law. They ensure the path of asceticism through meditative means. They seem to enjoy freedom diligently and volunteer to help others.

It is interesting to observe that unlike the nuns who have had experienced *Dukkha* in their lives and taken shelter in a nunnery to find a solution, the monks do not depend on such internal (अज्झत्तिकानि) experiences but are sometimes led to a monastery owing to their external (बहिरानि) experiences. Talaputto-Thera, in his former life, was an artist, very sincere and serious about his profession. He always believed that an actor when devoted to his former life was an artist, very sincere and serious about his profession. He always believed that an actor when devoted to his profession (by making people laugh and enjoy) would enjoy heaven after his death. He met the Buddha who told him that he was following wrong views (मिच्छादिट्ठि), and might go to hell. Hearing this Talaputta was so shocked that he started weeping. Similar was the case of Aṅgulimāla, a dacoit who followed the Buddha to kill him. As he could not reach near the Buddha he asked him to stop. The Buddha said to him "oh Aṅgulimāla, I have stopped, but you have not, you should stop". (ठितो अहं अङ्गुलिमाल, त्वञ्च तिट्ठा "ति आह ।). Hearing this, he was confused and sought for an explanation. Thus we notice that some monks, after receiving a sudden jolt or shock in their lives, have renounced the world. In such cases the ego of the person is hurt; there is no feeling of submission but subjugation. However in the process of monk-hood they have gradually learnt that सब्बं दुक्खं ! (all is suffering).

III

King Menandros or Miliñd of Sāgala has his roots in Greece (Bactrīa). A foreigner by birth he was a true, faithful disciple of the Buddha. He was a philosopher and a great exponent of Buddha's doctrine. His dialogues with monk Nāgasena reveal a tinge of the Greek (Plato) style. The debates consist of inferences, analogies, dilemmas and syllogistic reasoning. One can notice that the approach and attitude of *Miliñd-Pañha* is different from those found in the books of *Khūddaka-nikāya*, namely, *Therigāthā* and *Theragāthā*. Both are written at different levels. We must remember that the gāthās of the monks and nuns are entirely devoted to the Buddha's faith and teachings and in the case of King Miliñda, as a wise house-holder, possessing the power of a Kingdom. He does not take anything for granted as a monk or a nun would do. He is more discerning and truthful. He first makes a proposition, followed by an argument to find out the pros and cons of the point. This is a very different but a more interesting approach than that of Theras and Theris.

The questions about 'Dukkha' were asked by King Milind , which one finds very interesting, appealing and erudite. The scope of the subject becomes two-fold as it pertains to a householder and a recluse. The attitude of the former is worldly, mundane and the latter is more philosophical and missionary. Both participants are proficient in their fields and therefore the dialogues become significant and impressive. Now, let us examine some of the questions.

In *Miliñdapañh*, wisdom (*Pañña*) is considered as a basic factor for the realisation of Dukkha. There a question was asked, "what are the characteristics of wisdom (भन्ते नागसेन, किं लक्खणा पञ्ञा। The monk Nāgasena answered, "wisdom, for it is the one that cuts (छेदनं), enlightens (ओभासनं). After the rise of wisdom (पञ्ञा) one can dispel the darkness of ignorance and realize the four noble truths which lead a monk to see an end of *Dukkha, anicca and anattā*." [20]

In other words it means to understand अरियसच्चानि (four noble truths) that wisdom is very necessary, without which one cannot end the Dukkha. A simile is given in this context namely, that when a lamp taken into a house which is dark, dispels the darkness and everything is made clear; similarly the darkness caused by ignorance vanishes with the help of wisdom (Pañña).

The next questions was : "oh Rev. one, where does the पञ्ञा go? The monk answered, 'wisdom (पञ्ञा) after giving rise to good-act, vanishes but the realization of suffering and end of suffering, impermanence and end of suffering, impermanence and anattā do not vanish".21

Here is a simile : just as a certain man, in the night calls a writer to write, by lighting a lamp and when the writing is completed the lamp is extinguished; but the writing remains. Similarly पञ्ञा vanishes but not the realization of दुक्ख or end of *Dukkha.*

Another simile is : a physician makes a medicine of five roots and cures a patient. Once when a patient is cured, there is no need of the medicine. Similarly पञ्ञा when active brings under control all the five of organs, along with their defilements (किलेसा[5]). After this act of पञ्ञा there is no need of पञ्ञा to exist. This means realisation and eradication of Dukkha will last till the end of one's life, without taking the help of पञ्ञा (wisdom.).

Again King Milinda asked, "Oh Rev. one, does a tranquilled one feel a pain of Dukkha ?[22] (भन्ते नागसेन, यो न पटिसन्दहति, वेदेति सो किञ्चि दुक्खं वेदनं 'न्ति ।) Answer is : "yes, sometimes he does and sometimes he does not" and the explanation given is - "He experiences physical pain (कायिक वेदनं) but not mental pain (चेतसिक वेदनं)". Again a questioon was asked, "How is it that such a calm one experiences the Pain of Dukkha? Can he not pacify it? "The answer is "No, oh King, for *Arhat* does not have repulsive or courtesy feeling for pain. He does not allow unripe pain to fall down, nor does he welcome that pain which is matured."

In short Arhat is indifferent to pain and therefore he is indifferent to *Dukkha*. He allows physical pain (कायिकं) to take its own course. Thus Arhat is not totally free from कायिकदुक्खं. The greatest example can be cited is that of the Buddha who in his last days suffered from dysentery but did not make any attempt to stop it.

King Milinda asked another tricky question "Oh Rev. Negasena, is good feeling (सुखावेदना कुसला वा अकुसला वा अव्याकता?) meritorious or demeritorious or indifferent ?[23] The answer was, "It can be all three". Again the King questioned "If that is so, if merit does not give rise to *Dukkha*; if *Dukkha* is not merit then why not merit (कुसल) end *Dukkha* and not give rise to *Dukkha*?"

The answer is given in a simile. If in one hand of a man a hot-iron ball is kept and in another hand an ice-ball is kept, then will not that man burn both his hands? "Yes he will." This means that both hot and cold can burn the hands; they cannot stop the pain. Similarly कुसल (merit) and अकुसल (demerit) can cause pain (दुक्ख).

Once King Milind asked, "Do you exert (वायाम) to get rid of *Dukkha* of the past? Or future? or present?" Rev. Nagasena said, "no, oh King' "If that is so then why do you exert ?" "Oh King I exert so that suffering should vanish and other *Dukkha* will not rise, for this purpose I am exerting.[24]

Again the King had questioned him, "Do you think that you would have Dukkha in furture (अनागत दुक्खं) and the monk said "No, Sire". "Then why do you exert for अनागत दुक्खं, which would not be there?" The monk explained to him by giving similes, as follows:-25.

" Oh King is there a possibility of your enemy who has been defeated by you, to wage war against you?" "Yes". "Then do you prepare yourself after his attack?" "No, we make preparations regularly including regular parades of elephants, horses, chariots, army etc; and this we do to avoid future dangers". "Oh King, just as you prepare yourself to face danger which is not there, similarly we monks exert ourselves for अनागत दुक्खं". The monk gives two other similes (a) just as one who does not start digging a well when one is thirsty but digs it beforehand, his future provision. (b) Or just as a man does not start ploughing his field when he is hungry but does it before and makes a provision for food. Thus an *arhant* has to be conscious and alert throughout his life to keep away from *Dukkha*.

King Milinda was well- versed in the Buddha's doctrine. Once he thought -It has been accepted that when one transgresses *Dukkha* he enters into the state of an arhantship; therefore the Question would not be : does *Dukkha* penetrate into the state of an arhantship therefore now the Question would be : does *Dukkha* penetrate into this state of spiritual bliss?

He questioned "Is *Nibbāna* complete happiness or mixed with Dukkha?[26] The answer was, "Nibbāṇa is complete *happiness* (एकन्तसुखं) and is not mixed.

King Milinda argued, " I do not believe it for I feel that it is mixed with sorrow. The reason is that those who have achieved *nibbāṇa*, suffer from bodily or mental torment. They squeeze all the spheres of the five sense organs (पञ्चिन्द्रियं) and thereby close them, cut all the forms of pleasures. Thus they torment their body and mind; owing to this they suffer from bodily pains (कायिकदुक्खवेदनं) and mental pains (चेतसिकदुक्खवेदनं). For this reason I say that *Nibbāṇa* is mixed with *Dukkha*".

Rev. Nāgasena argued, "No, you are mistaken, Sire, you talk about the earlier phase of निब्बाणं , the state when one is striving to obtain *nibbāṇa*, but when once he experiences it, then it is only complete happiness and not mixed with *Dukkha.*" He gives a simile : a King who before obtaining a Kingdom has to fight with enemies, travel in the storm or jungle where mosquitoes bite, animals horrify, but once he becomes a ruler he enjoys only the happiness of Kingship and there is no suffering, no sorrow, at this state. Similarly *nibbāṇa* is a state of complete happiness, not mixed with Dukkha.

He further explained [27]- *Nibbāṇa* is complete happiness and not mixed with *Dukkha,* for *Dukkha* is one thing and *nibbāṇa* is another thing (अञ्ञं दुक्खं, अञ्ञं निब्बाणं). For this he gives the example of a teacher : Teaching gives happiness to a teacher but before becoming a teacher he has to undergo many troublesome duties. This part of life is his earlier (पुब्बभागे) and sorrowful duty. But when he becomes a teacher he enjoys the happiness of teaching- It is only सुखं with no mingling of दुक्खं । So is निब्बाणं only एकन्तसुखं only happiness.

Thus we observe that the points raised in Miliñda-pañho are partinent, intellingent and human. The debate between the two wizards starts with the questions based on a subtle level of philosophy and often ends with apt analogies. The book discusses *Dukkha*- suffering by taking into account *Pañña, Vedana, Kāyika-vedana-sukha, Cetasika Vedana- Sukha,* etc., but falls short of showing a path that would lead to end sufferings- *Dukkha*. One may feel that King Milinda is giving a let-out to the doubts of the common-discerning man. Perhaps the debate on *Dukkha* may not lead to the root cause of suffering but it certainly enlightens us to know the boundaries of the subject which eventually imparts more knowledge about *Dukkha*.

References

1 Dr. W. Winternitz, *History of Indian Literature*, Vol. II Calcutta, 1933, p. 111.

2 Prof. N.K. Bhagwat, *Therigātha*, University of Bombay, Publ., Bombay, 1937, p.p. ii- iii.

* She is a rare example of a woman in Buddhist literature who had to marry thrice.

3 Aññatar ā Bhikkuṇi, *ibid.*, p.8.

4 *Ibid.*, p.13.

5 *Ibid.*, p.12.

6 *Ibid.*, p.16.

7 *Ibid.*, p.5.

8 *Ibid.*, p.15.

9 *Ibid.*, p.17.

10 *Ibid.*, p.21.

11 *Ibid.*, p.27

12 *Ibid.*, p.9.

13 Prof. N.K. Bhagwat, Theragatha, University of Bombay Publ. Bombay, 1939, p.54.

14. *Ibid.*, p. 56.

15. *Ibid.*, 73.

16. *Ibid.*, 112.

17. *Ibid.*, p.122.

18. *Ibid.*, p.90.

19. *Ibid.*

20. *Ibid.*, p.37.

21. *Ibid.*, p. 42.
22. *Ibid.*, p. 44.
23. *Ibid.*, p. 44.
24. *Ibid.*, p. 89.
25. *Ibid.*, p. 90.
26. *Ibid.*, p. 287.
27. *Ibid.*, p. 288.

Concept of Dukkha in the Buddhist Nikāyas

17

Parineeta Deshpande

Suffering as a feature of life on this earth is too obvious and familiar to need description. Suffering is but universal. A great deal of human suffering is what we term roughly physical pain as well as mental and moral. In all ages the pressure of this problem of pain has been felt. It may even be said to be the driving force in all philosophy and in every religion. The classical example of the solution of the problem of pain is the doctrine of the Buddha. 'Suffering I teach, the way out of suffering' the Buddha declared. Thus, his root-focus is on the down-to-earth fact of human existence and not on any metaphysical questions.

We have the Buddha's teachings in the doctrine of the Four Noble Truths, which was the subject matter of the first sermon [1]that he preached to his original core of disciples in the Deer Park at Isipatana. These Four Noble Truths are nothing else but the cardinal articles of Indian Medical Science applied to spiritual healing, exactly as they are in the Yoga Philosophy.[2] That the Buddhists themselves were not ignorant of this fact is clear from their calling the Buddha 'The Great Healer'[3],the Healer of the entire universe (*sabbalokatikicchako, Mahābhisakko*). It is a significant fact also that Vāgbhata, the famous Indian writer on Indian Medicine, salutes Buddha as the Primeval

Doctor in the opening stanza of *Aṣṭāngahṛdaya*.[4] Vasubandhu, the commentator of *Abhidharmakośa,* recognises this fact.[5] Now, when we speak of Dukkha Ariyasacca, this very epithet of the Buddha is very relevant. He was indeed a spiritual healer who discovered the melady of suffering, sought for its cause; having resolved upon its cure sought for the good medicine of Nirvāṇa.

Note that in the enumeration of the Four Noble Truths, effects are put before causes. The first and the second Noble Truths represent respectively the effect and cause of *samsāra*. The third and the fourth truths (the cessation of suffering and the truth concerning the path leading to the cessation of suffering) are respectively the effect and cause of *Nirvāṇa*. The first two truths are characterized as Sāsrava (soiled with passion, fraught with defilement) and the last two as *Anāsrava* (Pure and conducive to *Nirvāṇa*, free from difilement). From this, it is evident that these are not truths in the ordinary sense of the word. However the Buddha spoke of them as the '*Noble truths*' - *ariya Sacchāni*. This means that they are not merely epistemological or rational truths as the word means. The concept of nobility involves a value judgement. Here the term 'noble' implies, as it has been said in the *Samyutta Nikāya*,[6] relevance or worth fruitful (*atthasaṃhita*) while the ignoble (*anāriya*) is defined in term of the fruitless (*anātthasamhita*). This is the original Buddhist manifesto. It contains the roots of the whole, complex tree of Buddhist religion and philosophy. And in spite of its comcept of Noble Truth it is based on human perspective, its relevance to human life. The pragmatic concept of the 'Noble Truth' presented by the Buddha is, therefore, not only epistemologically relevant but also ethically significant. Among this morality has its place and there is a mild lustre of Buddhist ethics.

In spite of its immense variety of doctrinal remificatiions, Buddhism is but one common vision of reality. The whole of Buddhism is mounted on the wheel of 'suffering'. No 'suffering' no Buddhism. Being a radical empiricist and a pragmatist, the Buddha, taking the bull by the horns, dealt with the riddle of existence without indulging much into the philosophical speculations. Therefore his first priority has to recognize the fact of suffering that pervades the psycho-cosmic reality of life that is Dukkha. The term is traditionally translated into English as 'suffering'. But, though it certainly includes this concept, it possesses a wide spectrum of connotations besides. Etymologically 'du' means difficult and 'kha' means to bear. So, at one extreme it takes in the most dire forms of mental and physical pain and anguish someone who falls a prey to total despair. It covers our everyday aches and pains, our dislikes and frustrations too and it extends to the very subtle feeling of malaise that life is never quite right.[7] So I think the organizers of this seminar have also given the original Pali words as the theme of this dialogue and not following its English rendering. The Sutta has made already a differentiation between the transcendental notion of *dukkha* and such particular, concrete manifestation of pain as lamentation, grief, despair, etc. The use of the term '*Dukkha*' in describing the world of objectivity is more appropriately understood as 'unsatisfactory' than as suffering and the reason for considering an object 'unsatisfactory' than as suffering is that it is impermanent and subject to transformation (*Viparināma dhamma*). The *Saṁyutta Nikāya* (21.2) tells us - "All formations which constitute the individual stream of existence are transient (*anicca*); all such formations are subject to dukkha; all things are without a self-substance (anāttā).... That which is transient is not worthy of our attachment. Ultimately no true happiness can be desired from that which is so ephemeral and so leads to suffering. Thus the three fundamental characteristics of individual existence according to Buddhism known as three marks *trilakkhaṇa* are philosophically relevant as they point to the very root of suffering. Anicca, represents the transiency and impermanence of all objective manifestations of beings in the realm of existence, including all the corporeal reality which constitutes the embodiment and support (*aśraya*) of all mental actions.

Anāttā-represents the subjective side of impermanence as this mark points to the insubstantiality of what appears to be an absolute and permanent ego; thus it signifies the total absence of a commonly postulated ontological basis of our mental and willing functions. Thus the wheel of *Dukkha* turns around this bi-polar axis of world-impermanence and ego-insubstantiality. Suffering, therefore, is rooted in the metaphysical characteristic of existence as radically impermanent and non-substantial.

Notice, however that the Buddha is not saying that there is only dukkha. He certainly does not deny the light side *sukkha* is not. At the same time there is no such thing as perfect unalloyed happiness (except Nirvāṇa). Even the most beautiful experience has a melancholy undertone simply because we know that it can't last. So Dukkha touches everything that exists. Happy things do come to us in course of events and should be enjoyed while they last. But we tend to want only happiness and, resisting all else, pursue it exclusively and cling to it desperately.

So the beginning of the road to wisdom is with a realistic and not pessimistic realizatioion of the fact of *Dukkha*. The Buddha's analysis of the Dukkha took him back to the point of birth. If birth has initiated a problem that eventually ends in death, every effort should be made to minimize the '*dukkha*' that a human being experiences between birth and death. Birth in the past and now, I set forth just this, *Dukkha* and cessation of *Dukkha* (M.I.140). When the first sermon summarizes its outline of *dukkha* by saying, "In short the five groups of grasping are dukkha' it is referring to *Dukkha* in the subtlest sense. The five groups of grasping (*Upādāna Khandhas*) are the five factors which go to make up a 'person'. Buddhism holds, then, that none of the phenomena which comprise personality is free from unsatisfactoriness. Each factor is a group or aggregate of related states and each is an object of grasping (*upadāna*) so as to be identified as me myself.

To aid the understanding of *Dukkha*, details of each of these five factors are given. The first is rūpa-material shape or personality. The remaining four personality factors are all mental in nature. *Vedanā*-feeling, *Saññа*-perception, *Saṇkarās*-constructing activities and fifth is *Viññāna*, consciousness. Just like the term chariot is used to refer to a combination of wheel, shaft, axle, etc., we similarly use the term 'man' to these psycho-physical forces.[9] Grasping these five aggregates as the possession of one's ego is *dukkha* as they provide the basis of craving and desire (*Taṇha*). The five aggregates (*Skandhās*) are therefore primordially *Sāśrava*, soiled with passions. The same thought is expressed in *Dhammapada*

Sabbe sankhāra dukkhāti yada paññāya passati
Atha Nibbindati dukkhe, esa maggo visuddhiya

Dhammapada-278

Dispositions are certainly subjective yet the Buddha is here referring to certain objects that have come into existence to satisfy the dispositional tendencies in human beings. Such objects are called dispositionally conditioned *sabbe Sankhāra dukkhā"*. For example, all the facilities enjoyed by a sovereign king such as palaces, ports, pleasure gardens are dispositions according to the Buddha and eventually came to decay and destruction.[10] Being impermanent and dispositionally conditioned if one were to be obsessed by them, clinging to them as one's own, one would eventyually experience suffering. The unsatisfactoriness of the dispositionally conditioned phenomena (*Sankhāra*) lie in the fact that they leave the mistaken impression that they are permanent. This fallacy is the root cause of all *dukkha* in the world. The Buddha's advice to *Kaccāyana*[11] brings out very finely how *avidyā*-ignorance of this fact gives rise to dispositions and that eventually to an entire mass of sufferings to desire.

The second noble truth informs us that *Dukkha* has an identifiable cause that is *Taṇhā*, which is literally translated as 'thirst', but in fact possesses the same kind of spectrum of connotations as *Dukkha*. It is that fundamental ache that is implanted in everything that exists, a gnawing dissatisfaction with what is, and a concomitant reaching out for something else. So we can never be at rest but are always grasping for something outside ourselves. This is what empowers the endless cycle, driving us from one moment to the next, one life to the next. Here too resides our native clinging to existence.

But this can be avoided by understanding the true nature of life in the light of knowledge of the first Noble Truth of *Dukkha* which is the corner-stone of Buddhism.

References

1 *Dīgha Nikāya* - II 304, *Vibhāṅga* 99, *Samyutta Nikaya* (V.421 ff)

2 Vyasa's commentary on the 19 th Aphorism of second book of Patānjali's *Yogasūtra* (परिणामतापसंस्कार) यथा चिकित्साशास्त्रं चतुर्व्यूहं रोगहेतुरारोग्यं भैषज्यमिति एवमिदमपि शास्त्रज्जचतुर्व्यूहमेव तद्यथा संसारः संसारहेतुर्मोक्षो मोक्षोपाय एवेति।

3 Theragatha, *Buddha caritam* XIII.61.

4 यः पूर्ववैद्याय नमोऽस्तु तस्मै ।

5 Vasubandhu on *Abhidharmakośa commentary chap*. VII.

6 *Samyutta Nikāya*, 5.421 ff.

7 T.W. Rhys Davids' *Pali-English Dictionary* also comments that there is no word in English covering the same ground as *Dukkha* does in Pali. Our modern words are too limited and too specialized.

8 *Vinayapiṭaka*. I.3, Dh. 118,194,381, S.N.383, D.1.4, *Dhammapada*. 233.

9 *Miliñdapañha- Chakkana Pañha*, page 5, Bombay Edition, 1972.

Yatha hi angasambhara hoti saddo ratho iti,

Evam Khamnesu santesu loti satto'ti sammuti.

10 *Digha Nikāya,* 2.199.

11 *Samyutta Nikāya*. 2.16-17- *Kaccayanagotta Sutta*.

Contributors

Dr. C.L. Prabhakar taught Sanskrit and Vedas at Hindu University of America at Florida, USA.

Prof. S.K. Pathak, a well known Tibetologist, was attached to the Deapartment of Indo-Tibetan studies, Visva-Bharat. He has published several books and research paper on Tibetan language, literature and culture.

Prof. Pradyumna Dubey is the Head of the Department of Pali and Buddhist Studies, Banaras Hindu University, Varanasi. Prof. Dubey is a well-known scholar on Buddhist Philosophy.

Dr. Narendra Kumar Das teaches Tibetan Language and Literature at Visva-Bharati, he is also a sound scholar of Sanskrit and Prakrit languages.

Dr. J. Sitaramamma teaches in Nagarjuna University, Andhra Pradesh.

Prof. Bhagchandra Jain, former Professor and Head of the Department of Pali and Prakrit, Nagpur University and former Professor and Director, Jain Studies, Rajasthan University, Jaipur, is an eminent Indologist and scholar of oriental studies of India.

Dr. Dilip Kumar Mohanta teaches philosophy in University of Calcutta, Kolkata.

Dr. Bimalendra Kumar teaches Pali and Buddhist Studies at Banaras Hindu University, Varanasi. He has published several research papers on Buddhism.

Dr. Bela Bhattacharya is a renowned scholar on Pali and Buddhism. Presently Dr. Bhattacharya is working in the University of Calcutta.

Dr. Parineeta Deshpande is the Co-ordinator at K.J. Somaiya Centre of Buddhist Studies, Mumbai.